Cover Picture

The Portrait of the George, depicts the hotel as travellers would have seen it, from the early 1700s to the present day.

The exterior has not been altered apart from the Main entrance. This was the archway through which carriages passed into the courtyard, to unload the passengers and their luggage, until the 1840s.

Keepers of the MONARCH of old Inns

The George of Stamford

Author Ken Ford ©

Copyright © 2006

Published by Mad Publishing

First printed in 2006

ISBN: 0-9553292-0-5
      978-0-9553292-0-3

For information regarding this publication contact
Mad publishing at 36 Coggles Causeway,
Bourne, Lincolnshire, PE10 9LL
Tel: +44(0)1778 426084
Website: www.madpublishing.co.uk

Cover image, water colour by June Ford
Design and layout by Mad Publishing
Colour reproduction by Mad Publishing
Images by Foto 45 ©
Printed in the United Kingdom by The Magazine
Printing Co. Enfield, Middlesex.
www.magprint.co.uk

Contents

Keepers of the MONARCH of old Inns

Acknowledgements

I would like to thank David Landry, Chris and Mary Pitman and Nadine Bentley of the "George of Stamford" for their help.

Jon Culverhouse and Dr R.M Canadine, of Burghley House for providing me with tenancy records and for their invaluable help.

The Stamford Museum staff for the use of their indexes and pictures.

Stamford Library staff who kept us supplied with microfilm copies of the Stamford Mercury, also books and papers, during our research.

The Town Hall and Bob Williams for the access to their documents and books.

Bourne Library staff who obtained books relevant to my research.

Karen Tomlinson library assistant to the RAC for their records.

I would also like to thank people who sent me pictures, menus, and other information - Yvonne Parkhouse, Sue Bradford, Mrs J.Brudenell, Jan Potter, Lorna H. Hale and Tony Kirkman.

Thanks to my wife, June, for helping me with all the research, scrutinizing and correcting the text, and for painting the cover picture. I wish to thank my daughter Barbara and her husband Stuart for the colour photographs, also for compiling and publishing the book.

Introduction

Living in Stamford for the first 65 years of my life, I have naturally been interested in the trade's people who lived and worked in the town. Amongst our own Stamford ancestors we have found Inn keepers, a hairdresser and umbrella maker, an ostler, coach trimmer, and going back to the early 1700s, a tailor and a long case clockmaker.

Researching these gave me an appetite to find out more about other Stamford trades people, resulting in publishing the book "Who Traded Where."

Stamford has always had a large variety of Inns, public houses, cafes and restaurants to cater for local people and the travellers who have used the Great North Road, on which the town has stood for centuries. It is with this in mind that I decided to research and write about one of England's oldest and most famous Coaching Inns, "The George of Stamford."

In writing I wanted to show something of the people who worked at the Inn, and it hasn't been easy as most of them spent their lives working to make ends meet, not many had the time or inclination to write about everyday happenings. Perhaps they did not think later generations would be interested. Some of the Innkeepers have been difficult to find.

I do hope that the people mentioned along the way therefore will be of interest and perhaps ancestors of yours. If we have missed anyone out, or made mistakes about their names etc., I do apologise.

Life does keep on repeating itself: Through the centuries there were transport problems, floods, ice and snow, robberies and confidence tricksters. Staff marriages, and even an under ostler sold his wife. Bankruptcies, deaths, a murder and a suicide. Wars, peace celebrations, coronation celebrations, and the list goes on.

In December 2003: The traffic in Stamford is brought to a halt, and pauses, to allow a mail coach and horses of a bygone era to continue on a memorable journey. Under the Gallows once more after a Stirrup Cup stop at the very old and famous George Coaching Inn. The Royal Mail coach and those four magnificent white horses came from, Peter and Caroline Dale-Leech's Red House stables and working museum in Darley Dale, Matlock, Derbyshire.

THE GEORGE OF STAMFORD

Foreword

On the banks of the Welland valley, in the South West corner of Lincolnshire, there stands the ancient borough of the Town of Stamford.

The beginnings of the town are lost in the mists of time, but its picturesque beauty still remains as it endeavours to keep pace with the ever changing demands of modern times.

Although the greater part of the town is in Lincolnshire it does border on to Rutland in the West and on the South by the county of Northamptonshire, now called Cambridgeshire.

A traveller entering Stamford from the South will be seeing a similar scene to the coaching days of the 18th and 19th centuries.

Many of the buildings in the High Street St. Martins, date back to the 18th century and earlier. The railway bridge halfway down was not there until the 1840s of course, but as you pass St. Martin's church on your right, there was a row of shops down almost to the town bridge.

In front of you the famous gallows sign of The GEORGE HOTEL, spanning the Great North Road. It was erected in the early 1700s and is a picturesque reminder of the bygone coaching days as a welcome to the honest traveller, but as a warning to the Highwayman.

It is one of only a few remaining signs of this type in England.

The George Hotel stands at the bottom of the hill, on the left hand side.

It is geographically in Northamptonshire, lying just south of the river, which is the border between the two counties. Now called St. Martins Baron, or Stamford without, it was in olden times called, Stamford beyond the bridge.

The early years

The GEORGE Inn

Historians have referred to it as The Monarch of old Inns, and a very ancient hostelry. Travellers in the 1700s reckoned that the Inn was, "The largest and finest in all of England."

I have found a reference to cumenhus, which is an Anglo-Saxon word for Inn. The Inn was said to have been built around 922 A.D. to 947 A.D, but there doesn't seem to be any definite evidence. At this time the land south of the river Welland was being used by the Saxons for building. A bridge would have been erected to span the river, as previously people would have crossed at the ford, further along Water Street.

The Inn was built on an ideal site situated in the valley, close by the bridge and on the edge of the town.
With the back looking onto green pasture land and meadows, it remained like this until the building of the railway in the 1840s.
It must be over 1,000 years old and as far as we know it has always been known as The George, after St. George, the patron saint of England and his association with the Knights of the Holy Sepulchre, and not as some people believe after George the King of England!

During the 1100s at the rear of the George Inn, now the courtyard, a person by the name of Siward who we believe was the Provost of Revesby Abbey, built a handsome church. Now this may seem a strange arrangement today (a church and an inn together) but in those days an inn was a place where travellers to the church, also other people passing through the town would be able to stop and get a good meal, shelter and a bed for the night. Ale and beer drinking taking place in the taverns and ale houses in the town.
The church has long since disappeared except the vaults, in which the wines are still kept in ideal conditions. The old burial ground could have been where the Monastery garden is today.

As there never was a Monastery in St. Martin's area, some romantic individual called it so, because the garden is pleasant and peaceful to walk through, or just to sit and forget those everyday worries and cares.
The old gnarled mulberry tree is over 250 hundred years old, and may date back to the reign of James I. It was he who imported mulberry trees in the early 1600s, with the idea of creating the silk weaving industry. He had made the mistake of ordering the dark flowered variety, instead of the white flowered ones, as it is the leaves of this variety that the silk worms feed on.
However the fruit of the dark flowered mulberry tree produces a delicious berry, which can be made into mulberry pie!

The sunken garden would have been a carp pool and later in the 1700s was turned into an excellent bowling green. Nowadays during the summer months, a large marquee is erected on it for wedding receptions and many other outdoor events.

We know that in the past there was an orchard containing a variety of fruit trees to provide the Inn's requirements, part of which today, is the Hotel's car-park with spaces for over 100 cars.

In one corner there was a piggery, a very useful disposal unit for the food left over from the kitchen and dining rooms of the Inn. Then the animals would in turn, have become prime pork joints, bacon, ham, pork dripping etc.

A good size kitchen garden and greenhouses would have been used to grow a large proportion of the hotel's vegetables, which in those days of self sufficiently was essential.

The farm, provided beef and mutton, also eggs and poultry. Game was plentiful in the local area and in years gone by the pigeon was a favourite dish.

A good supply of oats and fodder would be available for the horses stabled at the George, during the coaching era.

In those early days the Inn would have been a smaller building than today, standing together with the adjoining properties of St. Thomas' hospital, on the north side near the bridge. Then on the south side, was the Hospice of the Holy Sepulchre that covered a large part of St. Martins, up to Church Street. The properties were maintained by the Augustinian Canons of the Holy Sepulchre from 1150 to 1189 and subsequently by the monks of Peterborough Abbey.

Here might be found pilgrims and the Knights of the Military Orders on their way to, or returning from, the Holy Land. The Inn catering for all travellers, whether they were on the King's business or the clergy, or indeed for private or personal reasons. All of them would be needing food and drink, and somewhere to rest overnight on their journey along the Great North Road.

In those early days the Inn would have been a smaller building than today, but still catering for the travellers who were mainly on the king's business or the clergy and other church representatives, and all of them needing food, drink and a bed to rest overnight.

Travelling before the mid 1600s, could only be achieved by walking, or by riding on horseback. Men had boots, spurs, saddles, bridles and good riding suits before setting off on a journey. Gentlemen would ride with swords and pistols, riding in one suit and carrying a second to wear at their journeys end. Ladies who travelled needed safeguards and hood, side saddles, panniers with strappings, saddle cloths which were either laced or embroidered. Riding was more of a necessity than a pleasurable pastime.

Ladies sometimes rode pillion, that is one behind the other for companionship and also for safety.

After many hours in the saddle the rider would look forward to the welcome of a good Inn or hostelry, where there would be good food, a roaring fire, and a bed for the night.

The next morning over breakfast with fellow travellers, a number of them would plan to ride together, sometimes with a guide and as protection from the menace of the highwaymen who often lay in wait for the unwary traveller.

We don't have proof that highwaymen visited the George, but they were known to frequent the Inns and sometimes get information from servants by offering bribes. After a robbery they would make their way to a better class inn, since they believed that such places were less likely to be searched by the constables.

15th to the 18th Century

It was in 1461, during the civil war between the houses of York and Lancaster that a troop of Lancastrians and other men under their leader Andrew Trollop, entered the town and destroyed buildings, entering churches taking away books, chalices, crosses, and anything of value. They destroyed the town's charters, documents, records and part of the ancient hospital adjoining the George was damaged.

There are no signs of the Inn itself being damaged, perhaps it was used by them, as a headquarters and certainly somewhere to eat and rest.

With the town's documents and papers being destroyed, this may be one reason why we have not been able to find any earlier landlords other than John Dickens, or Dicons (this was an earlier spelling of the name).

John Dickens was a wealthy and well known merchant who kept the George Inn from about the 1460s, he also kept another inn, this was called the Tabard which was also in Stamford, along Scotgate. He was involved in the affairs of the town and held the position of Alderman or Chief Magistrate of Stamford, in 1476, 1483, and 1493. John and his family, together with his Ostler, William Thacker and other staff, would have endeavoured to satisfy their guests, as the George was already an important and well known Inn on the Great North Road.

When the towns aldermen held their feasts, they were entertained by the town waites.

These were musicians who wore cloaks and silver collars, they carried a scucheon, or shield of silver. He kept this in safe keeping for use on these occasions. It may have been John who donated it to the town. It was later passed down to his son-in-law David Cecil.

With the increase of people attending the animal and Mid-lent Fairs and Markets in Stamford, this enabled the George and other Inns to flourish, with the town overflowing with people especially during fair weeks.

There were bands of travelling players and musicians who would entertain visitors and locals in the Monastery garden at the George or in the pasture land at the rear of the Inn.

John Dickens daughter and heir, Alice, was courted by David Cecil, a gentleman from Herefordshire. He was Bailiff to the Abbots of Peterborough who owned a large portion of the town and St. Martins, including the George and other Inns. David lived in the manor House at Tinwell, and you can imagine that when he came into the town on business or to see Alice he would ride his horse from Tinwell and across the meadows to Stamford and the George, which is situated near the river.

They were married at St. Martins Church in St. Martins Stamford in about 1489, and lived for some time at the Manor House in Tinwell.

David was left an interest in the George and also the Tabard Inn by his father-in-law John Dickens. The Inn-keeping trade was very good in those days, and David continued in this line for some time. Like his father-in-law he was elected as an Alderman of the town three times, in 1504, 1515 and 1526 and later on he became one of King Henry VIIIs Sergeant at Arms.

David Cecil had a son Richard, who in 1539 obtained the grant of the site of the recently dissolved priory of St. Michael as well as the church and 299 acres of land lying in the parish of St. Martins. He was also given a yearly allowance for repairs to be made to the George Inn.

Richard Cecil was father to William Cecil, the first Lord of Burghley, the great Elizabethan statesman, whose descendants are still seated at Stamford, in nearby Burghley House.

In 1560 Queen Elizabeth I granted all of St. Martins to Sir William Cecil, this of course included the George Inn, a very valued possession of the family, which they held for over four hundred years.

Although Queen Elizabeth was entertained at Burghley by Sir William Cecil, we cannot find any mention of her staying at the George.

One of the first landlords of the George Inn that we have found under the Cecils, was Andrew Scarre. We see that Andrew was an Alderman of the town in 1550, and in 1568 he was granted a licence to sell wine. When Andrew died in May 1584, the business was continued by his widow and his son William Scarre until the end of the century.

The Inn provided the family with a good standard of living as we can see by William's will in 1594 that he left his three Gedney cousins £10 each, three Gedney nieces £10 each, also gifts of land and 2 fillies to his friends.

There was mention of an infant son, but the main beneficiary was Anne his wife, who I imagine continued keeping on The George for some time.

A section taken from William Scarre's will.

In Andrew Scarre's time at the Inn, during 1570, there was a great flood which caused much damage to the George and surrounding properties, it also washed away the north end of the town bridge. The bridge was rebuilt by Lord Burghley.

It was in 1597 when Lord Burghley built the alms-houses on the north side of the George, just before the bridge, that he gave the landlord of the Inn the right to nominate one of the inmates, and this privilege still continues to this day.

It was also at this time that he rebuilt the East block of the Inn, fronting onto the High Street, and his family coat of arms can still be seen over the front door. An Elizabethan stone mullioned lattice window in the upper storey on the north side of the main block dates from this time.

The present spacious entrance, would have been a cobbled carriageway through which the coaches reached the picturesque courtyard, and the travellers would have rested in the general reception room, or in those days it was called, the Parlour. If the coach was making a dinner stop, then they would eat in the dining parlour. The kitchen was at the rear of this part of the Inn and it contained an astonishing collection of kettles, pots and pans of brass and copper, there were of course brass candlesticks and tongs etc. Also iron griddles, frying pans and steamers, arranged on shelves or hooks around the walls.

In the early 1600s the government established a series of Post Houses on the Great North Road at about 10 mile intervals, between London and Berwick. These were for the use of officials on government business, and it was the duty of each Post Master to see that horses were available at each stage. The George Inn was one of the first to be established and the landlords or Post Masters as they were called received a retaining fee of between six pence and three shillings a day. They were also allowed to let out horses to other riders on private business, and if necessary provide a guide.

When King James I made his way south from Scotland in 1602 he passed through Stamford, with a multitude of Noblemen, Courtiers, Sergeant-at-Arms, Gentlemen, Pages, Trumpeters, among others. All of them would need food and lodging.
The Inn was very busy with the local gentry and others coming into town to stay and see their sovereign. When his Majesty processed through the town the streets were packed with folk all eager to get a glimpse of the Royal parade, many people on stilts to get a better view. The Alderman, Tobias Lovedaye and his brethren attended him on horseback, riding on their foot cloths and the common councilmen in their gowns.

Royalty was to visit the town again in the 1630s and the 1640s, King Charles I made a number of overnight stops at the George, especially during the civil war of the 1640s.
The letter overleaf shows how the postmasters were commanded to prepare for his Majesty's visits.

This is the translation, written by the Court Secretary, Sir Henry Vane, to the Landlord of the George Inn at Stamford in the year 1640.
It refers to one of a number of journeys made by King Charles I during his reign, when he travelled either from London to the north, or when he was returning home and dined, lodged overnight or rested and changed horses at the Inn.

Can you imagine the planning that the Landlord, together with the Alderman of the town. would have to do in just a couple of days to carry out the King's command. Providing food and lodgings for the King's retinue, arranging the assembly of all those horses required and returning the horses that his Majesty and courtiers had arrived on.
Notifying the local nobility, would have meant dispatching messengers on horseback to the local villages and summoning their presence, there was no easier way of communication in those days.

~~~~~~~~~~

Whereas his Majesty intends to ride in post in three days from hence to the city of York, and sets forward on Thursday 20th August 1640 of this month; And to the end his Majesty and his servants attending him may at all stages and places where they shall dine, lodge or take fresh horses, be readily furnished with extraordinary good and able horses, geldings and mares to carry them along together, with fitted expedition.
These are therefore in his Majesty's name strictly to charge and command you immediately upon receipt hereof, repair to the Justice or Justices of the peace near you: And by virtue hereof to require their best assistance in sending to such noblemen gentlemen and others near and hereabout, requiring them to furnish, bring in and have in readiness at such place or places where his Majesty and servants shall lodge, dine or take such horses. One hundred good and able horses,

mares and geldings well fitted with all the necessary furniture. All such horses are to be brought in the night before his Majesty cometh: and to stay there till they have done the service as the owners own charge, who are to receive from them that ride them the prizes (payment) usual for such services.

In homage whereof this shall be your warrant wherein you are not to fail as you will answer the least neglect at your utmost peril.

Given at the court of Oatlands, the 17th of August 1940. Signed H. Vane.

P.S. These horses are to be ready on Thursday night, 20 especially for those who attend nearest the Kings person, and 6 more for my own use,

For his Majesty's special service
To the Postmaster of Stamford
Haste this & etc

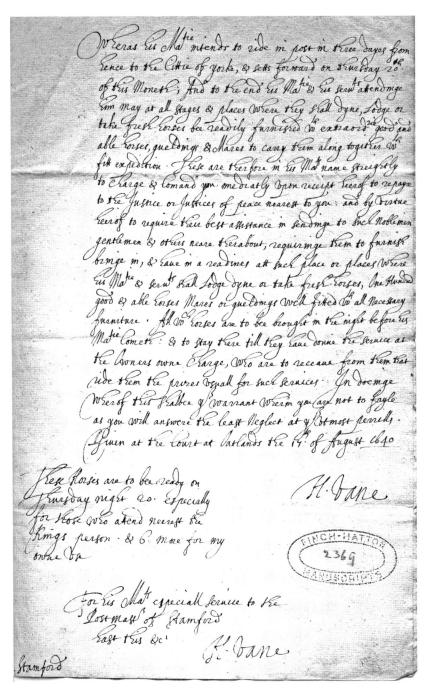

We found this important document when we were researching documents held by notable families in the area, and are now stored at the Northamptonshire Record Office. We have printed it with their kind permission.

In 1632 the town council gave the King a present of, a silver and gilded cup to express their devotion, (and gave orders that all houses on both sides of the street through which the King would pass, to be white washed). His majesty spent the night at the George, and the next day he journeyed on to Scotland to receive the crown of that kingdom.

The Corporation of Stamford escorted him through the town in procession. John Atton the Alderman, bearing the mace before him on horseback, attended by the whole corporate body in their robes of office, and riding upon their foot cloths.

The next year 1633 he stayed again, but in 1634 King Charles I was accompanied by Queen Henrietta.

It was on the 15th March 1641 that he spent another night at the George: this was when he was on his way to Grantham.

In April 1641, just after King Charles I had stayed at the Inn, a heavy fall of rain and a high west wind caused the river Welland to overflow and it flooded the streets near to the river. The ground floor of the George was under several feet of water and some of the horses were drowned in the stables, one of the stables collapsed and a horse was seen swimming around in the yard.

King Charles stayed again in 1642 this time he was on his way to York.

It was on Saturday 23rd August 1645 that King Charles and his army entered Stamford and he made his quarters at the George, his soldiers, making free of the town! After staying over night, he then continued with his army on their march from Newark to Huntingdon.

Although royalty and titled families were beginning to own and run coaches, the first stage coach to leave London for the North seems to be in April in 1658. They ran from The George Inn at Alders-gate London taking two days to reach The George Inn at Stamford, then continuing to York arriving two days later. It is difficult today to imagine taking four days to travel two hundred miles.

The coach ran on Mondays, Wednesdays and Fridays, from April and throughout the summer, but they were taken off the roads in wintertime.

These early coaches did not have any glass in the windows, instead there were shutters and leather curtains. The first coach to be fitted with glass windows was the one used by the Duke of York in 1661.

After spending some considerable time going through references of Alehouse and Innkeepers in the mid 1600s, there is a mention of a Robert Butcher, who was an Innkeeper during the 1650s. His will in 1670 shows that he was a man of considerable wealth, leaving his children money and property. He leased some property from the Earl of Exeter, but there is no mention of the George.

During the years 1665 to 1666, when London was being ravaged by the Plague, the town council felt it had to take drastic measures to prevent Stamford becoming contaminated.

A meeting was called and they voted unanimously to post one Alderman and two Burgesses to refuse admission into the town to all coaches, horsemen or travellers who had journeyed from London until the plague subsided. All Innkeepers, victuallers and householders in the town were ordered not to entertain or lodge any of these people. This must have caused hardship to the George and indeed the towns trade for some considerable time.

I have been told that there is a bedroom at the George where, a king was entertained by a mistress when he was in the district. My research has not revealed who the king was, but Charles II had quite a reputation for being entertained in this way, also he enjoyed getting away from London to

Newmarket for the races which were held there twice a year. Did he stay at the George and visit the Stamford races in the 1600s? We may never know!

Looking through the St. Martins Parish church registers for any information on the landlords and staff at the Inn. We found an early record of a Richard Ford buried on the 4th October 1676. He was a Tapster, which was a barman at the Tap Room of the Inn. He rented the room from the landlord. It had a door on to the street through which the local people came in to drink, separate from the Inn's travelling guests.
I don't know if Richard was one of my ancestors! As the Ford family were living in the Stamford area in the early 1700s.

William Wildman was the landlord in the 1680s and the food he offered in those days besides roast beef, turkey, tongues and salmon, were also partridge, woodcock, pigeon pie, larks, oysters, sturgeon and other delicacies.

Antonio Verrio was a guest at the George Inn in about 1688 for sometime – he was an Italian painter who was born in 1639, at Lecce nr. Otranto on the heel of Southern Italy.
Antonio was commissioned by King Charles II to paint ceilings in the royal apartments at Windsor. The antiquarian Ralph Thoresby mentions that he admired the delicate painting of the apartments particularly in St. George's Chapel, when he was travelling in that part of the country.
Then in about 1688 the Earl of Exeter employed him for about 12 years to paint the ceilings of the State Rooms, one of them being the Heaven Room and also the ceiling of the Grand Staircase, at Burghley House. During his employment at Burghley the Earl allowed him a coach and horses, together with servants, and when he could afford to, he stayed at the George Inn, where he ran up quite large bills living in style! There was a game of sconcing, it was drinking large amounts of ale without stopping, poor Verrio did not excel at this, so he frequently lost large sums of money. All this was in William Wildman's time.

The Town cleaned up several streets in 1696 to prepare for a Royal visit by King William III. Preparations also went ahead at the George Inn where his majesty stayed, he went to see the new palace that Lord Cecil had built at Burghley. He thought the building was a truly noble and magnificent seat, with such fine paintings. He was said to have remarked that, " it was too great for a subject."

When the coaches started running there were still some travellers who preferred to journey on horseback. One such gentleman who was a regular customer at the George during the late 1600s and early 1700s was Ralph Thoresby. Ralph was born in Leeds in 1658 and was the son of John and Ruth Thoresby a merchant of Leeds.

As an Antiquarian, Ralph travelled the country and made a number of journeys to and from London. In 1680 as they were entering Stamford from the north, a cart being driven furiously down the hill hit his maid's horse, her clothes being caught in the cart which brought her to the ground, fortunately she was not dragged under the wheel but sustained some injuries. After resting and eating at the George, they were able to continue their journey.

He came to the town again in 1683 and in the evening he went into St. Martins church to transcribe a memorial to Lord Burghley (you could just imagine his servant holding a lighted candle for him as there was no other illumination). Afterwards they dined and retired for the night. He mentions five handsome churches and two hospitals. The hospitals were the almshouses of William Browne in Broad Street and the Burghley almshouses next to the bridge in St. Martins.

Two years later he passed through again, stopping at the George where he baited! This was an old northern word meaning to stop for refreshment on a journey.

There was one journey on horseback when they were delayed by the atrocious weather. On December 29th 1708, during their ride from Grantham to Stamford they were subjected to gale force winds and heavy snow which caused drifting, each rider having falling from his horse, without any damage to themselves. They were delayed and could only get as far as Stamford, where they were pleased to find the warmth of a fire and good food. He had a Scotch physician as a chamber fellow, with so many travellers being stranded, there were not enough single rooms for everyone. Normally Ralph would have preferred to pay extra for a single chamber, with his own key and amply supplied with clean linen. Here he would have been able to sit and write or read, without any interference.

Next day there was no movement of coaches or horses because of the large quantities of falling snow and drifting. It appears that the day before had resulted in four or five coaches overturning. Ralph Thoresby was only able to get as far as St. Mary's church and back with the weather being so severe. Quite a number of people were stranded at the George and he speaks of good company in the evening, among them his good friend Mr Clark the rector of Somerby nr. Grantham, a physician, a lawyer and a major.

On the 31st, still unable to travel they went to All Saints church, then up to William Browne's Almshouse, and called at Mr Truesdale's Almshouse which had just been erected in 1700.
The following day he was feeling dejected but found some comfort in reading two or three psalms in secret. No one was willing to even think of travelling in this weather and Ralph was troubled by the loss of time and money!

It wasn't until Monday 3rd January, that he heard of some Scottish gentry who had been stranded with him at the Inn and they must of necessity be in London to attend Parliament at a time appointed, so he was at last able to continue his journey. There was 14 horsemen, this included a guide, who set off into the drifts eventually finding some parts better than others.

His last journey in March 1723 was by coach were he stayed overnight at the George, and on the return journey in June he lodged at the Inn where he hoped to meet up with Francis Peck, the curate of Kings Cliffe, but Francis was absent through sickness. It was Francis Peck who wrote The Antiquarian Annals of Stamford in the 1700s.

During the long, cold and dark winters there was not a lot of travelling, but when the spring arrived and the coaching season began again, it was considered to be quite an event. The first coach of the season would be, be-decked in garlands of flowers and ribbons. The coachman's whip stock was ornamented with coloured ribbons and bunches of flowers, whilst the coachman wore a large floral nosegay. The guard's post-horn was wreathed in flowers, and the horses too wore new harness and saddle-cloths, with wreaths of laurel on their heads.
The town music, which nowadays is known as the Town Band, and many of the residents would be there to welcome them as they drove into town.

Some of the Inns laid on quite a spread providing the coachman, guard and all of the passengers with gingerbread, plum cakes, homemade bread and biscuits. Ale, fruit wines, cherry brandy and sometimes spirits, and all of it free.

The notices on the following pages, are as they would have been written in the 18th Century, when the letter f was sometimes used for an s.

Coach travel time had not altered in the early 1700s. In April 1706, the York coach set out from the Black Swan in Holborn London at 5am every Monday, Wednesday and Friday, taking two days to reach the George Inn at Stamford and another two days to reach The Black Swan in Coney Street York. The coach was still running a Spring to Autumn service.

YORK Four Days Stage-Coach.

Begins on Friday the 12th of April 1706.

ALL *that are defirous to pals from London-to-York, or from York to London, or any other Place On-that Road; Let them Repair to the Black Swan in Holbourn in London, and to the Black Swan in Coney ftreet in York.*

At both which Places, they may be recovered in a Stage Coach every Monday, Wednefday and Friday, which performs the whole Journey in Four Days, (if God permits.) And fets fourth at Five in the Morning.

And returns from York to Stamford in two days, and from Stamford by Huntington to London in two days more. And the like Stages on their return.

Allowing each Paffeager 14lb weight, and all above 3d. a pound.

Performed By	*Bejamin Kingman,*
	Henry Harrifon,
	Walter Bayne's

Alfo this Notice that Newcaftle Stage Coach, fets out from York, every Monday, and Friday, and from Newcaftle every Monday, and Friday.

In the St. Martin's parish registers of the early 1700s, there were some servants from the George who had died there, only name and burial dates are given.

Thomas Simpson, May 1703. John Higgins, February 1705. Thomas Sturdy, April 1707. William Shaw, September 1707.

There were also some coach passengers Hector Jones, June 1700. John Ives, March 1701. John Pauley, February 1702. Mary Harrison, (a poor child), November 1703. Abraham Sheriff, January 1704.

In 1707 there was rejoicing and a wedding feast at the George, when William Wildman was married to Rebecca Lloyd, on the 27th June at Tansor parish church. She was from Tansor in

Northants. Rebecca helped him to run the Inn until December 1714 when William died, then we believe she continued on her own for some time to manage the Inn.

Throughout the history of the George there have been robberies, and at least one conman, but during the early 1700s there was a violent murder.

It was in 1714, during William Wildman's time at the Inn. He rented the Tap Room to a Mr Bolton who was sympathetic to the Jacobite cause. It was customary to drink to the memory of Queen Anne, kneeling and bare headed. It was when he was in the act of doing this that one of Honeywood's Dragoons, who were stationed in the town, plunged his sword into Mr Bolton's heart and killed him on the spot.
The Inn was suddenly surrounded by an innumerable crowd of people armed with all sorts of domestic weapons: they broke all the windows and threatened to demolish the Inn unless the delinquent was given up. The villain, however, escaped by the back way and the crowd gradually dispersed.

In 1717 The Earl of Exeter, who was very fond of horse racing, falconry and all outdoor sports, built a new racecourse, just about a mile south of the town, on the old North Road, even though there had been a racecourse on the site since the early 1600s.

The Straight Mile on the new course was reckoned to be one of the best in England. As the years went by the reputation of the Stamford racecourse grew and during race weeks the town came under siege, with race goers arriving by coach, on horse back and on foot. The distinguished guests stayed at Burghley house, but the George Inn was always bursting at the seams along with the other Inns.

In August 1721, there was a notice that Daniel Wallis who was a vintner (a seller of wines) lately of Kings Lynn in the county of Norfolk, now keeps the George Inn St Martin's, Stamford. He gives notice to all Gentlemen and others that he has, new wines of all sorts, this years growth, besides a large quantity of Old Ports, with French wines, Burgundy and Champagne to be sold at reasonable rates. Allowances will be made for large quantities. Also Right German Spa Water will be sold all this summer, in flasks.

Daniel Wallis, Vintner, that lately came from Lynn in Norfolk, keeps now the George Inn, in St. Martin's Stamford Baron, Northamptonshire, giveth notice, to all Gentlemen and others. That he hath lately come in a Parcel of new Wines of all sorts, this Years growth, besides a large Quantity of old Ports by him, with French Wines Burgundy and Champaigne, &c. Sold by the aforesaid. D.W. at reasonable Rates, Allowances will be made for large Quantitys. N.B. Right German Spaw Water will be Sold by the same Person all this Summer in Flasks.

August 1721

ON Sunday the 26 of this Instant, a Leather Portmanteau was taken out of a Coach in the George Yard in Stamford, Having in it these following Things, viz an Olive coloured Coat, Wastecoat and Breeches, a yellow and white striped Callimanco Night Gown, several Books and Writings, which are of no Service but to the owner. Whoever will give Notice of the same to the Master of the George Inn in St. Martin's Stamford, or to the Master of the Black Swan Inn in Holborn, London (so as they may be had again) shall have 2 Guineas Reward and reasonable Charges. If they have sold the Cloaths, and will return the Books and Writings, they shall have a Guinea Reward and no Questions ask'd.

August 30 1722

In the 1720s, Daniel Defoe, the author who will always be remembered for his popular children's book "Robinson Crusoe" amongst many other works, was travelling throughout the country and writing about the cities and towns that he stayed at and passed through.

It was during one of his journeys in 1724 that Daniel visited Stamford and he remarked about the very busy market, and the good trade the inhabitants enjoyed. He stayed overnight at the George Inn, out of curiosity, as it was reckoned to be, "The largest and one of the greatest Inns, in England". As he doesn't make comments on the hospitality of the Inn, we can only presume that it was of its usual very high standard.

He does however mention the state of the road north of Stamford as being in the clays which could be dangerous to travel in some seasons. The turn-pike charge seems to be about 3d for a coach about that time.

During the years of 1724 to 1726 the Earl of Exeter had the whole of the east front re-faced and thoroughly repaired. George Portwood, who was Mayor of the town in 1741, and well known for his trade as a Stone Mason, carried out the work. The repairs to the woodwork carried out by Robert Pilkington, a well known and respected joiner in the town.

This is the front of the main building as we see it today, placed in the centre of the parapet is a stone panel with side scrolls, bearing the arms of the Cecil family. There are two lead rain water heads, one of these also has the Cecil family arms on it. Over the centuries as alterations have taken place, the Inn still retains the thick walls, which although they are visible inside the building only add to the cosy and comfortable feel as you enter the lounges, dining rooms and bars.

There were strict rules on the selling of Ales, the aldermen of the borough appointed one of its members as official Ale-taster. In the 1720s Richard Rogers, a Freeman of the town and a constable was appointed to this position. It was he who picked out the inns at random and he would go into the tap room to sample a glass of ale. He checked the ale to see that it had been properly brewed and did not contain sugar or impurities.

I have also heard of an Ale–Tester. Wearing a pair of leather trousers he would enter an Inn unexpectedly and draw a glass of ale. Then pour some of it on a wooden bench, and then sit down in the middle of the puddle that he had made. There he would sit for 30 minutes by the clock. He would converse, he would smoke, he would drink with all who asked him to. But he would be careful not to change his position in any way. At the end of half an hour he would make as if to rise, and this was the test of the ale.

For if the ale was impure, if it had sugar in it, the testers leather breeches would stick fast to the bench, but if there was no sugar in the liquor no impression would be present. In other words, the tester would not stick to the bench.

I leave you to decide on the authenticity of this account.

There was a change of landlord at the George Inn during March 1725, when Jonathon Smith, who had lately kept the Bear Inn at Reading in Berkshire, moved into Stamford.

As the Inn was nearing completion of the work carried out to the exterior, its interior had been newly furnished and Jonathon and his staff were ready to entertain persons of quality and others with good usage! He also sold a full market measure of corn in the stables.

THE George Inn in St Martin's

Stamford Baron, Northamptonshire, being the largeſt and beſt in Town, is kept by Jonathon Smith, late of the Bear-Inn at Reading, Berkshire, is juſt now new furniſhed; therefore is ready for the Entertainment of Perſons of Quality and Others, with good Uſuage.

N.B. He ſells full Market Meaſure of Corn in the Stables.

March 1725

In April of the same year there was a notice that the Bowling Green at the Inn was now open and in very good condition. How did they keep the lawns trimmed in those days? It would have been tedious work with a scythe, or did they use sheep to crop the grass very short as the lawn mower was not invented until the 1800s. In fact, the lawn mower was invented in 1830 by Edwin B. Budding, who was an engineer from Stroud, Gloucestershire. After he had seen a cutting cylinder mounted on a bench which was used to trim cloth, to make it smooth after weaving, he realised a similar idea could be adapted for cutting grass.

A Market Ordinary, was available on Mondays if required by the gentlemen, after they had played Bowls. This was a meal provided regularly at a fixed price.

It was in 1725 that the Earl of Exeter had a cock-pit built by George Portwood in the area now part of Station Road, it was a very large building with a seating capacity for 600 spectators, measuring 40 feet across. Constructed from local stone and built in an octagonal shape, matches were regularly fought on the mornings of race days. The cock-pit was ready in the summer of 1725, and the Inn was advertising cock-fights during the Stamford Race week.
During this time the Hunters plate would be on show at the Inn. This annual event proved to be very popular and brought substantial business to the George and also to the town.

The Annual Stamford Race week in 1728 was started on the 11th June, which was Whitsun week and there would be the usual cock-fights in the mornings of the races and an Ordinary would be served at the George on the race meeting days.

Jonathon Smith appears to have run into financial difficulties, as we found that by Lady Day 1729, (March 25th) he was in arrears for the sum of £208.00.

It was in June 1728, when there appeared an advertisement.

> *To be Lett and Enter'd on at Midfummer next, or fooner, if required,*
>
> *THE George - Inn in St. Martin's near Stamford, Lincolnfhire, lying upon the great Northern Road, being a very large, handfome, and convenient Houfe, with Cellars, Stables, Barns, Granaries, and other Out-buildings, fuitable, and all in good Repair, being lately beautified and thoroughly repaired: There belongs alfo to the faid Houfe a Bowling-Green and Cock-Pit. And there will be Let with the fame, if defired, a Farm, containing a Sheep Walk, fome Inclofure and Arable Land and Meadow, all at very moderate Rents. There if alfo to Let at Wothorpe near Stamford, a Houfe with good Stables, Out-houfes, and other Conveniences at about 6 Pound per Ann. And alfo the water-Mill at Thorpe on the River Welland, and a Wind-Mill at Liddington near Uppingham in Rutland, with a Dwelling Houfe and other Conveniences.*
> *For farther Particulars enquire of Mr Richards at St. Martins near Stamford aforefaid*
>
> *June 1728*

The next landlord that we found to take the lease of the George, was Matthew Richars. This was in September 1730, for the Inn he paid a rental of £134.00 per year, also taking on the Lodge Farm, Water Close and Haines Close, for a further payment of £50.00 per year.

On the 5th April 1733 this notice appears. Whereas it has been falsely reported that the George Inn was, Shut up! This is to satisfy all persons that there is the same accommodation and good usage as usual. Signed Matthew Richars.

The Mercury in 1733 advertised a cock-fight. At the George Inn there will be fought on the 21st May next, and the following two days, a main of cocks between the Right Honourable Earl of Exeter and George Heneage Esq. to show 31 cocks of a side for 10 Guineas a battle, and 200 the main, and 21 cocks for bye-battles.

STAMFORD PLATES. We thought this notice on the Stamford Races was worth recording.
Note: A Plate, was a Cup or a Trophy.
On Tuesday the 12th day of June 1733: Will be run on the new course near Stamford. A Plate of Forty Pounds in Value, called the Town Plate, by any horse carrying 10 stone weight. Three heats, a contributor to pay 1 Guinea, a non contributor 3 Guineas entrance. If but one horse, starts, the owner to pay 10 Guineas towards the next years plate. No horse to run for this plate unless a certificate is produced under the breeder's hand, that such horse is no more than six years old at the time of starting.
On Wednesday the 13th June: Will be run on the same course a purse of Twenty Pounds, by Galloways. Three heats, 9 stone weight, a contributor to pay one guinea, a non contributor 2 Guineas entrance. If only one horse starts the owner to pay 7 Guineas towards the next years Galloway Plate; and the winning horse to be sold for Fifty Pounds.

On Thursday 14th June: Will be run on the same course, a purse of 80 Guineas. Three heats, 10 stone weight by any horse a contributor to pay one guinea, a non contributor 5 Guineas entrance. If but one horse enters, the Guineas will not be run for, but the owner of such horse shall have 10 Guineas for his charges and his entrance money returned. No horse that has won a King's Plate shall run for this purse. If any dispute arises for any of these three prizes, to be determined according to the several articles.

On Friday 15th June: Will be run on the same course, a purse of 20 Guineas. Three heats, 12 stone weight any horse. No person to enter more than one horse and that must be his own. Every horse to pay 2 Guineas entrance.

There will be cock-fighting at the George Inn every morning during the races; and any gentleman may send in what cocks they please.

N.B. At the aforesaid Inn there is accommodation for persons of the greatest distinction and there will be an ordinary served on the days of the cock-fights.

> *This is to give Notice,*
>
> *That the Lincoln Stage-Coach sets out from the Angel in Lincoln, every Monday and Thursday and takes up passengers every Tuesday and Friday from the George Inn in St. Martins, Stamford Baron; and goes into the Three Cups in Alderfgate street, London, every Wednesday and Saturday Night. Likewise sets out from thence every Monday and Thursday, and performs the Stage to Lincoln in three Days. A Glass Coach, or any other may be had with Horses upon the least Notice given to Mr John Vinter, or Mr Thomas Youick, who performs the aforesaid Stage.*
>
> *August 1733*

There was more cock-fighting on the 26th to 27th February 1734, the fights were between the Gentlemen of Rutland and the Gentlemen of Lincolnshire. A market ordinary would be served on both days.

On the 29th April 1734 the Bowling Green had been thoroughly renovated and was opened and ready for the seasons matches.

The second theft took place just before Christmas. Stolen from the George Inn on Sunday 22nd of December, at night, one light-coloured cloth coat with metal buttons, a flannel waistcoat, a pair of strong jockey boots, with one inlaid with a spur, one pair of double channelled pumps, little the worse for wear but have been heel-pieced.

The person who stole them is a low old looking man, he walks stooping, and had on a very bad horse-hair wig, a dark coloured coat, a new light coloured Yorkshire cloth waistcoat with metal buttons, and grey yarn stockings. Whoever secures the person shall have a Guinea reward, that's £1.05. Paid by Mr Matthew Richars at the said Inn, or if any of the said goods are pawned or sold, he will return them their money again, and reasonable charges at the delivery.

A notice on the 27th February 1735: Any person wanting clean rye grass seed:
It may be obtained from Isaac Rayner of Apethorpe - or samples can be seen and seed ordered at the George Inn, Stamford.

Matthew Richars became a Bankrupt in 1735, with debts totalling £1000 – goods to the value of £352 were seized. An inventory shows virtually no furnishings but included:
Wine Vault:
1 Hogshead of Red Port, and 1 of White Port. 12 gallons of Rhenish (Hock), and a further 24 of Old Hock. 5 doz bottled Cider. 2 doz of Tent (Alicante wine). 1 of Arrack(a coarse spirit). 1 of Rum. 8 of Red Port. 1 of Canary. 1 ½ of French claret.
Ale Cellar:
5 pipes of Ale. (a pipe was a large cask) 5 Hogshead of Ale. (a hogshead is 54 gallons). 12 doz. bottled Ale.
Small Beer Cellar:
Six pipes of small beer. 36 doz small beer in bottles, 27 Hogshead. And a half of all thralls (these were the timber stands on which the barrels were placed).
The linen amounted to 482 pieces in all, including Damask and Huckaback, the napkins included "11 with Black Crosses."
On the 5th June 1735 this notice appears;
Thomas Alcock, who keeps the Bull Inn St. Mary's Street, has now taken over the George Inn St. Martins as well, and welcomes gentlemen and others to the aforesaid Inn. During the forthcoming Race week, 10th June ordinaries will be served as usual.

When Thomas Alcock took over the Inn's goods to the sum of £723, he avoided taking over the farm, but rented Nun's Close. Thomas became Mayor of the town in 1737, and he only kept the Inn for a further 3 years, as by 1740 he had died.

A notice on 10th July 1740 states: Whereas Thomas Alcock who kept the George Inn, St. Martin's Baron is lately dead. This is therefore to inform the public that the said Inn will be kept by Brian Hodgson, his Son in Law. Where all persons will be sure of meeting with an agreeable entertainment. N.B. All person indebted to the said Thomas Alcock are desired to repay their respective debts to Brian Hodgson aforesaid.

I believe that the Hodgson family had kept the Swan and Woolpack in St Martins from the late 1600s. The Inn is now called the Bull and Swan.

Brian ran the George for about 10 years, he also took over the Farm, Nuns Close and the fields, together with a Cellar in St. Mary's Hill. (I think this wine cellar was near to the bridge).

Brian was a gentleman who enjoyed the sport of cockfighting, and challenged a Mr Hallam of Boston to a combat between their birds at his cockpit in St. Martins during May 1746.

His eldest daughter Margaret made a notable marriage, on the 13th May 1765 she married a clergyman, The Rev. Beilby Porteous, who eventually became the Bishop of London.

Brian Hodgson and his family left the George in the summer of 1750, eventually moving to take over the chief Hotel in Buxton, would this have been the Old Hall Hotel?

In 1745 King George II son, the Duke of Cumberland, who was also known as the Butcher, after his victory at Culloden over the Scots, stayed the night at the George. He may have stayed here on other occasions as well.

There was a brief visit by John Wesley in February 1746, who was one of the greatest evangelists in the history of the Christian Church, and founder of the Methodist Church in this country. He was travelling from Stilton to Grantham where he would be preaching that evening and the snow was falling thick and fast by the time they reached Stamford Heath (about a mile south of the town) where it was lying in deep drifts. Within the hour they were able to make it to the George Inn at Stamford, where they stopped for a short while to refresh themselves. Setting off again, the weather had not improved and they had to spend the night at Great Casterton.

The next landlord to take over the Inn was Marmaduke Skurray. An agreement was signed in September 1750 to take the George for a rental of £150.00 per year. The lease excluded the cockpit, but included the wine cellar at St. Mary's Hill and also the Farm and Fields etc.

Marmaduke and his wife Jane with their family moved to Stamford from Lincoln, where they had managed an Inn and I believe they were originally from Alford, a market town in the north of the county.

This old map shows the fields at the rear of the Inn, which were included in the lease of Marmaduke Skurray in the mid 1700s.

Stamford Races started on Tuesday 11th June 1765, which was another busy week for The George. Race officials, judges, and gentlemen from all parts of the country were staying at the Inn.

Marmaduke put on an Ordinary on the Thursday. As usual there was cock-fighting each morning, and that year it was between Mr Edward Wills and Mr Denshire. Forty cocks each on the main, and twenty on the byes. 10 Guineas a battle.

The George Inn had another royal visitor in 1768, when the King of Denmark who was visiting England, stayed over night as he journeyed around the country.

There was a spectacular event in the afternoon of 21st May 1772, which drew the crowds to watch the Royal Regiment of Horse Guards Blue riding into the town, down St. Martins to the George Inn. Commanded by General Conway, they had been reviewed on the racecourse to the south of Stamford, by General William Pitt, the younger. It was he who was to entertain the officers to a splendid meal at the George, superbly prepared by the landlord Marmaduke Skurray and his staff. The Horse Guards were stationed in the area until May 1773 when they returned to London.

In June 1772 on Stamford race week, there were four mornings of cockfighting at the George cockpit. Robert Piggott and Captain Sharpe's birds were fighting each other with sixty one cocks on each side, at 5 Guineas a battle. This was on Tuesday to Friday.
On the Thursday Marmaduke put on an ordinary, this was a meal provided regularly at a fixed price, usually on market days or special events.

We know that Marmaduke died in 1773, and we think his wife Jane continued to run the business until she died just two years later in October 1775. They were both buried in St. Martin's churchyard. Their family eventually moved away from Stamford and settled at Nottingham, where his son, Marmaduke died in March 1815.

John Terrewest was the next landlord to take over the George Inn at the beginning of 1776. He leased the Inn at £70.00 per year, also George farm and Boor's close, together with the Nun's closes and a meadow in Walcot Holme. The rentals for these were £105 per year, but John would most probably sub-let some of the pasture land.

It was in 1776 when he moved in with his wife Mary and their four children. Sadly he lost his wife Mary as she died in February 1777, leaving him to continue with the business and raise the children for the next seven years. Then John died on October 12th 1784, and was buried in St. Mary's churchyard.

When John Terrewest died he left a young family, the youngest child being Ann Tomlinson Terrewest aged just 11 years. Now the person who took over the Inn, farm and land etc., was a George Tomlinson. This set us thinking, the youngest child had Tomlinson as her middle name, so was George a relation and did he and his wife move in to bring up John's young family? Our research into this has not yielded any answers.
George Tomlinson leased the Inn for £70.00 per year. The farm, and land etc., for £120.00 per year.

The Ninth Earl of Exeter's building programme for the town in the 1780-1790s, was carried out on a number of his properties in the St. Mary's Street and St Mary's Hill area and included the George Inn. The east side, as we have mentioned was thoroughly refaced and repaired in the 1720s. The North wing was completely rebuilt in the 1780s, replacing what had been a wooden gallery on the first floor. This wing was to include the main dining room, kitchen and lodgings for the ostler, grooms, boots and other staff. It was completed in 1789 at a cost of just over £1000.

Then the south wing was rebuilt in 1791, two storeys high and over a large cellar. There was a room on the first floor used as an assembly room and anterooms etc. The cost of building this wing was £314. All of the south wing is now divided into bedroom suites.

There was an accident at the Inn during March 1785, when Christopher Fairchild a chaise driver for the George was killed by a kick from one of the horses. Christopher was buried on the 9th March in St. Martins churchyard and left a wife who was expecting their fifth child any day. On the 4th of April they had a Charity Card Assembly at the Inn, all donations to go to Christopher's widow and her five children, to help them in their bereavement.

A regular mail coach service was created in 1786 for the London to Edinburgh mail.
With the mail it carried four passengers inside and one outside, sitting next to the driver, and it was scheduled to travel at 8 mph. They used ordinary coaches in the early days, but eventually a more superior coach was developed.
The mail coaches always used four horses even if there were no travellers, and sometimes in very bad weather conditions they used six horses.

The coach driver was issued with a brace of pistols as they were easier to use when holding the reins, and the guard was issued with two blunderbusses, and were often ex-servicemen who where used to discipline. He was issued with a free uniform, the coat being a scarlet colour with gold braiding, and a black tall hat with a cockade. Another piece of equipment was his post horn, which was sounded upon the coaches departure and arrival, the post horn was eventually replaced in the early 1800s by the key bugle. This bugle came over from Germany and for a time displaced the old yard of tin, the earlier guards had blown so lustily. The new generation developed a passion for this new instrument, and many became experts playing cherry ripe, the huntsman's chorus and other popular tunes of the day.

I understand that the Royal Mail Coach did not pay tolls so the Toll keeper would listen for the mail coach horn and keep the gates open, as they had to run to a time schedule.

A travel announcement: The Royal Mail Coach, with a guard leaves from The Bull and Mouth Inn, Bull and Mouth Street, London at 9.30pm to arrive at the George Inn every morning at 8am, then continues on to Edinburgh.
The Edinburgh to London Royal Mail Coach calls at the George Inn at 3pm every afternoon and arrives in London early the next morning.

Towards the end of the 18th century the George was to change hands yet again. After just four years at the Inn George Tomlinson left and Peter Fawcit took over the Inn.
I believe he was a Yorkshire man from Cranthorne, the son of William Fawcit of that place. Peter and his wife Mary had been the landlords of the Saracens Head Inn at the High Street in Lincoln. They moved with their family to Stamford at Michaelmas (September 29th 1789).

When Peter took over the lease of the Inn the rental had increased to £100 per year. He also took over George farm, Nun's Close, Bull Close the meadow in Walcot Holme and a meadow in Uffington for £123.00 per year
They had only been at the George for five years when Mary died in January 1795, she was only 53 years of age, and was buried in St. Martins Churchyard.

A timetable of the coaches leaving The George in the 1790s: Stamford Diligence sets out from the George Inn every morning at 3am to the White Horse Inn, in Fetter Lane, Fleet Street, London. Returns every morning at 7am. The Newcastle Light Coach sets out from the George every night at 10pm to the Bull and Mouth Inn, London. Where it arrives at 10am every morning.
Returns at 7am to arrive at the George Inn at 6pm the same day. There is a coach to Newcastle,

which sets out every day at 5am. Then a coach from Newcastle sets out at 1pm every day (arrival times not given).

The George Inn became famous as a Coaching Post House, and it is said that there were at least forty coaches a day, twenty each way. There are two rooms inside the front door which are reminiscent of those days. On the left a door labelled London, it was here that the South bound passengers waited for the arrival of their coach or the changing of fresh horses in the court yard. The other room on the right was labelled York, for passengers travelling to the North.

With all that traffic, the courtyard of the Inn would have been a hive of activity. The Driver helping the passengers out from inside the coach, while the Ostler would have put up a ladder for the passengers travelling on the outside to get down. If it was a dinner stop they would have gone into the dining room with hopefully a blazing fire, if it was cold. The break for a meal was usually 30 minutes, consisting of most probably mutton broth, rich in meat and herbs, fresh water fish, eels stewed boiled or spitchcocked, this was an eel split and grilled or fried, and salmon.

There would be the finest saddle of mutton, done to a turn, Irish stew, rump steak, chicken or duck, followed by plum pudding, fruit tart and gooseberry fool. There was also a cold menu of beef, pork or ham, with a choice of cheeses and home baked bread. Ale or the best fine wines of a sound vintage kept in perfect conditions in the cellars.

Meanwhile in the courtyard, the Ostler, groom and stable hands would have had plenty to do harnessing the fresh horses and cleaning and feeding the ones to be stabled, then loading the passengers luggage and packets securely for the next part of the journey. The driver did not always travel all the way, so when he had finished his part of the journey he would go into the dining room of the Inn with his whip and hat in hand, to collect tips from his passengers. Is this what was called a Whip Round?

It was in the last quarter of the eighteenth century, when the Rev. Thomas Twining, who was a learned English divine, and on his travels stayed in Stamford. He wrote of the "distracting bustle of the George which exceeded anything I have ever seen or heard."

The well known Scottish romantic poet and novelist Sir Walter Scott who was born in Edinburgh in 1771 was a frequent visitor at the George. He made numerous journeys to London, travelling mostly in the spring. In 1799, he was accompanied by his wife Charlotte, and they struggled through heavy snow and bad weather in Scotland with the conditions improving as they journeyed south. It was Walter who wrote that the view of Stamford town, as you approached from St. Martins was, "The finest twixt Edinburgh and London." A view he often saw when staying at the Inn. I understand that on one journey in the 1820s his daughter Anne travelled with him.

Walter Scott gave an eloquent description of the appearance of stagecoaches in his time. They were covered with dull black leather, thickly studded with broad headed nails tracing out the panels. The heavy window frames were painted red, and the windows themselves provided with green cloth or leather curtains, which could be drawn at will. On the panels of the body were displayed in large characters the names of the places whence the coach started and wither it went.
The coachman and guard, (when there was a guard) sat in front on a high narrow boot, often garnished with a spreading hammer-cloth with a deep fringe. The roof rose in a high curve. The wheels were large and ill formed, and generally painted red. In shape the body varied. Sometimes it resembled a distiller's vat somewhat flattened, and hung equally balanced between the immense back and front springs. In other cases it took the shape of a violin/cello case, which was, past all comparison the most fashionable form. Again it hung in a more genteel posture, inclining on the back springs, in that case giving those who sat within the appearance of a stiff Guy Fawkes.

Before the railways came to this part of the country in the 1840s, the only transport was by horse or horse drawn coach, carriage or other horse drawn vehicles.

When a member of the titled gentry died away from their country seat the only way to convey them to their home was by a horse drawn hearse.

Monastery Garden

The area behind the shrubbery was the site of a chapel, if you walk about halfway along the left hand side of the Monastery garden, there is an opening. The doorway on the right being the building's entrance and this could have been used as a chapel of rest in the early 1800s.

On Wednesday evening 27th January 1804, the remains of the Earl of Ancaster lay in state on that evening. The next morning the cortege was conveyed in a solemn procession to Edenham church, near Bourne for a family burial.

The Chapel of Rest was used on Tuesday the 12th April 1808, when the remains of Sir Henry Grey rested here the night, on its way to Northumberland. The deceased was Uncle to Lord Grey.

It was in use again on Friday evening the 5th December 1811 when the cortege carrying the remains of Mrs Noel, an amiable Lady, the wife of Charles Noel MP.

She rested overnight, then on Saturday morning was conveyed to Exton village church to be interred in the family vault. Exton is a small village about five miles north west of the town.

Sunday evening the 10th November in 1816, the remains of Lady Hildyard rested at the George exactly two years after the remains of her husband, Sir Robert Darcy Hildyard, rested in the same room. Before the final journey on the next day.

The remains of the late Countess Fitzwilliam, Dowager Baroness Ponsonby, having been removed from Wentworth House on Thursday 9th September 1824, rested at the George Inn chapel of rest on Friday night. The next morning the funeral cavalcade proceeded to Marholm church near Peterborough, where the body was deposited in the family vault of the noble family which the Countess had been for a short time allied. Her Ladyship's marriage with the Earl Fitzwilliam took place in Ireland, on the 21st July 1823. She was born in October 1749.

Lady Sophia Heathcote's remains rested overnight on Wednesday evening 10th June 1825. The next morning the hearse proceeded to Normanton accompanied by three mourning coaches, and were followed by fifty tenants of Sir Gilbert Heathcote, all mounted on horseback. Her remains were then interred in the family vault at Normanton church.

The body of the late Countess Dowager of Pomfret, rested en-route from Richmond to Greatford. She was the daughter of the late Thomas Trollope Brown of Greatford. She died on the 17th September 1839 aged 70 years, and was interred in Greatford Church, where there is a memorial tablet.

The 19th Century

The start of the 19th Century, was the heyday of the Coaching trade, there was an improvement of road conditions and coaches became more comfortable to travel in. The 1820s saw Gas lighting in Stamford and other towns, which made life easier for the Hotels and catering trade, and eventually gas was used for cooking and then heating, although it took many years to establish. Then halfway through, the railways started to cover the country and with it, the decline of the coaching business, but more people were able to travel and the Inns became Hotels to cater for the rail travellers.

At the beginning of the 19th Century Peter Fawcit and his family involved the George Inn in a number of the towns activities, business and social etc. In the courtyard on the south side, there was a suite of rooms that were used for a variety of activities, private and public meetings, sales, auctions, and banquets.
During the elections it was also the headquarters for Lord Exeter when he was contesting his seat in Parliament.

The Commissioners for the Barholm enclosures held a meeting on the 4th August 1800, in one of the courtyard rooms, to discuss drainage and division of fields with the various landowners. Over the next few years there were many meetings for the villages surrounding the town, including Tallington and West Deeping, Langtoft and Baston, Easton and others.

We do have a number of "sponsored walks" and other events these days, mainly for charity.

In 1801 there was a PEDESTRIAL PERFORMANCE, this was for a 200 Guinea wager, (A guinea was £1.05 in today's currency).
On the 7th June 1801 a Cantab, who was a Cambridge University Student, left London at midnight, to walk to York (some 200 miles north) and arrive by midnight on Thursday 11th June 1801.
He had breakfast at the George Inn on Tuesday the 9th June, on his way to York. Then he arrived at York Minster on Thursday afternoon at 4pm, covering the distance with 8 hours to spare! Quite a feat, but I wonder who he or she was?

On the 11th June 1801 there was the theft of a strong rusty coloured mare, she was marked with a star on her forehead and had a bushy tail. A saddle and the bridle were also stolen. The saddle was nail marked with the initials HF. The thief also took the post boy's greatcoat and his whip.

In spite of the vigilance of the staff at the Inn, there was another theft of a mare from the stables. A man stole the mare on a Sunday night, in April 1804, the police however arrested him the next day. He was sent to jail at Huntingdon by John Heathcote, who was the magistrate of the court.

On August 27th 1804, a special evenings entertainment was promised at Stamford's Theatre in St. Mary's Street. It was for the benefit of widow Selby who was unfortunately left with 9 small children. A Miss Hamilton of the Theatre Royal in Bath, was going to perform part gratis. Tickets were available from the booking office at the George Inn. Boxes 3/-, Pit 2/-, Gallery 1/-.

D. Mardell, an Auctioneer held a sale of timber in one of the rooms in the courtyard at the George on the 2nd November 1804. The timber, owned by Mr Tatum was of oak, ash and elm trees standing in the woods and grounds at Essendine and Carlby.

An advertisement appeared in the Stamford Mercury:
A Gentleman leaves Stamford on the 24th December 1804, in a Chariot and four able bodied horses for Bath, via London. Accommodation for any Gentleman or Lady going that way.
Please apply to Peter Fawcit of the George Inn.

This would have been quite an arduous journey in those days I would imagine, as it was in the middle of winter.

There was a theft from a carriage, which had stopped at the Inn on the 21st December 1804. Francis Rawdon–Hastings, the 2nd Earl of Moira who was Master General of the Ordnance (dealing with military supplies). When travelling to London from the North, the Earl and his entourage called at the George, to have a meal and a rest. It was when his carriage was standing at the gateway that the robbery took place, no doubt the coachman and guard being distracted. A box and portfolio containing several valuable papers, besides money and other articles of value were stolen as well as a holster of a brace of pistols from inside his carriage. The box was found the next morning, broken to pieces and under a hovel in a paddock in St. Martins. Fortunately the papers were not destroyed and were returned to his Lordship, whose Aid-de-camp, Sir William Kerr arrived the next afternoon and returned to London with them.
A valuable miniature was overlooked by the thieves, but the other property they decamped with and they have not been arrested yet!

Three suspicious persons, who arrived at the Coach and Horses in St. Martin's a few days before the robbery absconded later that evening, having not reclaimed the horses they left at the Inn. The Inn mentioned was at No.19 St Martins which is the property immediately before St. Martin's church.
The box and papers were found by a poor boy, who was looking for hen's eggs in a paddock. He received a reward of 10 Guineas. That's £10.50 a small fortune in those days, and no doubt the family would have had the best Christmas feast ever! I wonder who the boy was?

There was an auction of the estate of the late George Tomlinson on Tuesday the 5th February 1805 at the Inn. George had been the landlord of the Inn from 1785 to 1789 as we have mentioned earlier.
He had invested his money in property in St. Martins, at the auction were two houses with outhouses, coach house, stable, yard and garden. In the occupation of Mr. Robinson and William Harper. A coach house and barn. In the occupation of Francis Weldon. A close of pasture land in the tenure of Edward Butt, being part of the cow pasture. This land was in the area where the Wothorpe Drifts are today, just of the Kettering Road. The solicitors involved were Messrs Jackson and Judd.

A close of rich pasture land of 1 acre 2 rood and 26 poles, part of the cow pasture St. Martins, was put up for auction at the Inn on the 25th January 1806 at 7pm. It was the property of Widow Holmes.

At about 6 o'clock in the evening on Sunday the 12th October 1806, their Royal Highnesses the Prince of Wales (who later became George IV) and the Duke of Clarence arrived at the George Inn. It was here that they took fresh post horses and proceeded on their journey northwards. Whilst his Royal Highness stopped at the Bull Inn on Witham common, a post boy driving hastily up to the Inn, stuck the pole of his chaise through a panel in the Prince's carriage. His Royal Highness without waiting for it to be repaired, proceeded on his route. Remarking with his goodness of heart that, "the incidence was trifling compared with the pleasure he felt, that the post boy's life was preserved."

An advertisement in the Mercury on the 16th December 1808: For Sale. Two strong Hunters, Eight years old, used to carrying 16 ½ stone, sound and perfect. The property of a Gentleman. For further details, apply to the Groom at the George Inn.

One of the suite of rooms in the courtyard was used by the Tax Inspector. A notice announces that the Inspector of Taxes will be at the George Inn from 10am to 3pm on the 15th January 1809, for Land owners and other tax payers to pay their dues or to lodge an appeal.

During the Stamford Race Weeks in the early 1800s a frequent visitor to the races and the George was Daniel Lambert, literally their biggest customer. He was born in Leicester on March 13th 1770 and as a young man was prodigiously strong. In his later years the muscle turned to fat, and when he died on June 21st 1809, at the age of 39, he weighed 52 stone, 11lbs. He was 5ft. 11ins tall, measured 112 inches around the body, and 37 inches around his thigh. He died at the Waggon and Horses Inn, Nos 48 to 50 High Street St. Martins. His headstone can be seen in the churchyard on Barnack road.

When Daniel travelled to London he lodged at the Kings Head, near the Stationers Hall Court. At that time it was a fashionable coffee and chop house. It was here that he held public receptions, at which visitors for a moderate fee, might look upon his fifty two stone of human flesh. After he died the tavern became known as the Daniel Lambert, and his portrait hung upon the walls. In the late 1800s the premises were acquired by a well known firm of caterers for a modern café, and the portrait put up for auction and fetched the sum of £5.10s.

This portrait now hangs inside the foyer of the George. It was painted by J. Parry in about 1804. Daniel's walking stick is also on view.
There is a permanent display of his clothes on a mannequin in the Town's Museum.

The Inn was busy too on Auction days.
On the 6th December 1809, seven lots of garden ground now in the tenure of Mr. Chapman were to be sold by the auctioneer, Samuel Mills between 3pm and 5pm.

Christmas 1809 was a very sad occasion for the Fawcit family as the master of the Inn, Peter Fawcit senior died just a few days before Christmas. He was 79 years of age.
Peter Fawcit junior took over the running of the Inn, with the help of his two sisters, Jane and Amelia, although I imagine they had been managing the business for some time. Besides the Inn Peter also had the George farm, which is just under a mile from the town, going south.

In January 1810 there had been a number of attempts to rob his farm, which was occupied by his farm workers. In one instance a villain fired a gun at one of Mr Fawcit's employees. They had tried to set fire to his haystacks too, one of the offenders was wounded by a gun shot as he tried to escape. There was a total reward of £176 for their capture.

French Prisoners of War Escape:
On the 18th April 1811, two French officers, General Excelman and Colonel De La Grange, absconded from Chesterfield prisoner of war camp. They were accompanied by an interpreter. Calling at the George they took post horses to Stilton. The alarm was raised and a constable pursued on horseback, but was unable to re-capture them.

In May 1811, Joseph Inman who had been a Waiter at the George – took over the Crown and Woolpack Inn at 51 Scotgate and advertised accommodation for Stage Waggons at the rear of the Inn.

It was on the 26th August 1811, after a days shooting at the range on the Stamford Race Course, which was about a mile south of the town, between The Duke of Cumberland's Sharp Shooters, The Artillery Company's Yagers, and The Nottinghamshire Riflemen. The Nottinghamshire Riflemen and the Yagers went to the George Inn, where a sumptuous feast and entertainment was in readiness for them. A buck had been very handsomely presented for the occasion by Sir Wollaston White. Bart.

Soon after the dinner Captain Bessell of the Yagers arose, and after a very neat speech, presented a handsome medal to the Nottinghamshire Riflemen, conveying the following well merited compliment on their conduct. "Presented on the 26th day of August 1811, by the Yagers of the Honourable Artillery Company, to the Nottinghamshire Riflemen, as a token of respect for the encouragement which by their late public invitation they have given to the useful practice of Rifle Shooting." On the other side, the Arms of The Artillery Company; motto "Arma Pacis Fulcra".

In the August of 1812 there was an Auction at the Inn, of the estate of Reuben Terrewest esq. I believe he was a relation of John Terrewest, who was landlord of the George in the 1770s. There were a number of properties sold, all of them were in St. Martins, and they were in the occupation of Rev. Mr Amphler, Zaccarhius Pollard and Mr Baxter.

During our research we have come across various incidences, and I think this is a very interesting one that involved the George Inn.

On Tuesday the 14th April 1813 a young man riding on a Bay Horse came to the Horse And Jockey Inn at Uppingham. He told the landlord, a Mr Catlin that he was going into town to receive some money, and requested the loan of 5/- for the purpose of facilitating the transaction. The landlord not suspicious of the trick intended to be practised on him, lent the money. Off his guest went, not however to pay off the borrowed sum, but to provide a cheap method of transport away from Uppingham.
Entering the Falcon Inn, in the town he ordered a chaise for Stamford, which was to meet him as soon as possible at the Toll Bar. He came to Stamford and went into the George Inn, where he ordered his supper and drank some Negus, this was a hot drink of port and lemon.
Then he went off into town on the pretence of transacting business, but alas, he did not return to the Inn. He unfortunately forgot! Ere he departed to pay for his supper, the Negus, the chaise hire and the post boy still waiting in the hotel courtyard.
The landlord at the Horse and Jockey Inn, Mr Catlin, had the horse on which the swindler rode into Uppingham. He left it with a note, found afterwards asking the landlord to let the animal be properly exercised etc., and he signed it Green esq, but the horse is supposed to belong to someone in Leicester.
Mr. Green was described as, a young man, about 5ft 6ins tall, rather jolly, light coloured whiskers, he wore a blue coat with yellow buttons, narrow corded breeches, white boot tops, and had very much the appearance of having been a gentleman's valet.

At about 3.15pm on Friday the 24th September 1813, an earthquake was felt in the town, there was a loud noise and the tremors lasted for just two seconds, but there was no structural damage caused at the George Inn.

The winter of 1813 to 1814 was a cold one with low temperatures causing the roads to freeze, which made coach and any travelling very difficult. The river Welland too was frozen over.
In the early 1800s, before the railways were built, all the land to the rear and side of the George down to the river, belonged to the Inn. A footpath from the rear went across a footbridge into the town.

About midday on February 11th 1814, William Kemp was clearing ice from the bridge when a large sheet of ice he was standing on broke in two, he fell backwards on one piece and was propelled downstream. Still holding a piece of wood however he was able to steer to the bank safely and get onto firm ground. A number of people saw the incident but were unable to help. As it turned out all ended well, but later on a part of the bridge itself was swept downstream.
After such a severe winter, the summer of 1814 was a scorcher! On Tuesday 18th June the temperature recorded in the afternoon reached 84 degrees in the shade.

The year 1814 was a time for rejoicing too, as Napoleon Bonaparte had been defeated and the war with France had ended.

Flags were flying at all the six churches in the town, and at various time during the day the church bells were ringing. The shops and Inns were all illuminated, they would have been lit with oil lamps, or like Peter Fawcit who lit up the sign across the road at the George Inn with candles, which had a most picturesque effect!

The town celebrated with a ball at the Assembly Rooms, with over 200 persons dancing into the late evening to the music of the Loyal Nottinghamshire Rangers from Norman Cross Barracks. From midnight to 2am the company retired to the card room to partake of an excellent supper which consisted of soups, fowls, lobsters, tongues, jellies and fruit, which was supplied in profusion by Peter Fawcit of the George Inn, and his sisters Jane and Amelia Fawcit to whom, the highest praise is due for their excellent management on the occasion.

One of the rooms in the courtyard was used as a courtroom in September 1814, when James Pearson and Francis Fardell, a Currier in the town were fined the sum of 5/- each for Hare coursing in the Easton Fields – they were brought before the magistrates, G.V. Neunberg and the Rev. Atlay.

The family were celebrating at the Inn on the 23rd September 1814, when Peter's sister Jane Fawcit was married to Richard Norris at St. Martins Church. Richard was an Apothecary and a Surgeon, who had his practice in St. Martins.

One of the suite of rooms on the south side of the George's courtyard was used by the Lawyers as a Bankruptcy Courtroom.

We know it was used three times in the early 1800s, Mr Wing, an Innkeeper had his bankruptcy hearing there in August 1805. The next year William Bromhead, who was a well known Ironmonger in the town went bankrupt in December 1806.
Then in May 1815, Peter Fawcit of the George Inn was declared bankrupt, with debts totalling £466.00. News soon spread around that the Inn would close, but this was quickly dispersed when a statement appeared that the business and posting of the George Inn would be carried on as usual.

Burghley House acted immediately to advertise one of their most sort after properties.
The George Inn of Stamford, is now to be Let, and may be entered upon immediately.

The Inn comprises of 10 Sitting Rooms and 38 Bedrooms; with a spacious Kitchen, Bar, Larder, Laundry and every other convenience. There is stabling for 86 horses, coach houses, a blacksmith's forge and extensive outhouses of every description. Also a large garden and orchard. At the back door are the river Welland, and about 17 acres of Pasture Land, in two closes.
The Inn has two entrances and is situated near to the bridge in Stamford, and is upon the Great North Road from London. It possesses all the advantages that can possibly belong to a large Inn, which has for a great number of years been resorted to by the first families in the kingdom. 17 pairs of horses in capital condition are daily employed in the above concern.
There is also a most desirable farm, containing 267 acres of arable land in the highest state of cultivation, to be let with the Inn. The above farm is on the North Road just under a mile south of the Inn. It has a Farm House, Stabling, Hovels and every convenience for occupation. The incoming tenant will also have the advantage of stock in trade and effects at a fair valuation, if he thinks proper. An opportunity to the above seldom occurs, as this is without question one of the first situations of the kind in Great Britain.
Apply to Mr Adams, Burghley House, near Stamford: *and if by letter pay the postage.*

Advert dated, 17th May 1815

For the race week at the beginning of July 1815, there was the usual cock-fighting in the mornings Tuesday to Friday. This year between the Gentlemen of Bedford and the Gentlemen of Warwickshire and there were 200 birds at 10 Guineas a battle.

On the 18th of August in 1815, there was a new coach on the York to London route. The coach was named The Prince Blucher, after Field Marshall Blucher, the Prussian Field Marshall who commanded the Prussian army against Napoleon at the Battle of Waterloo in 1815. The coach left York at 6pm arriving at the George Inn, Stamford at 8.45am, then arrives at The Bull and Mouth Inn London, in good time each evening.

There was a special dinner held on Friday 6th October that year.
Sixteen gentlemen, friends of Major Thomas Noel Harris of Whitwell, who had lost his right arm at the battle of Waterloo, gave a most excellent dinner to that gallant officer, at the George Inn. Sir Gerard Noel. Bart. was in the chair and he presented the Major with a large silver cup, as a mark of their esteem, and complimented him on the valour he showed in the various battles in which he had been engaged on the continent.
Major Harris we understand would be going the following Tuesday for France again to join Lord Stewart, and is entrusted with the four swords voted by the Corporation of London to the Commanders of the four armies of the Allies.

The assignees of Peter Fawcit (now bankrupt), held an auction at the Inn on the 20th October 1815. Selling a selection of posting mares, in pairs, post chaises and harness complete, all of them in good condition. There were also 8 blood horses, many acres of crops, swedes, turnips etc. Then on Monday the 5th November there was a sale of furniture, waggons and implements. Altogether quite a large and comprehensive sale, which would have attracted buyers from a wide area.

Peter Fawcit then moved away from the town, and according to reports he went to Grantham where he was employed as a book keeper at the Angel Hotel, Peter died at Grantham in September 1826, when he was just 46 years of age.

The next Landlord to take over the George Inn, (which had been left in a run down state by the previous tenant), was another Yorkshireman and farmer, Thomas Thompson Whincup. Thomas was born at Stockton-on-the-Forest in the 1770s, a small village just a few miles east of York. He was the son of Thomas Whincup who I would think was also a farmer. The family moved to Kirk Hammerton that is west of York, and it was here that he married Sarah Lawson in March 1798.

I understand from their descendants that Thomas and Sarah had a large family of 22 children, but we have some information on just four of them, two sons and two daughters who were born between 1800 and 1813. When Thomas and Sarah decided to take the lease of the George Inn, I would think it was a huge task with young children who were between the ages of two years and thirteen years. The children on the other hand would probably have been looking forward to a real adventure travelling nearly 120 miles by coach and to a part of the country they would have known very little about. The mail coach travelled at 8 miles per hour, but their journey would have taken longer as they would have had overnight stops on the way.

Sarah Whincup, the wife of Thomas Whincup
Taken about 1850

Their daughter Ann, who was born in 1800 was married to William Chapman of Stamford in 1825, and no doubt there would have been a wedding feast and celebrations at the George on that special day.

A descendant of Ann Chapman, Yvonne Parkhouse has contacted me and she told me that Ann's husband, William was a farmer and they lived and worked in the Harringworth area. When her great grandmother used to stay at the George as a child, she would play with her cousins on a flat roof.

Henry, the eldest son who was born in 1802 became involved in the Inn-keeping and Hostlery business with his father. Between the two of them, Thomas and Henry, they ran the George for nearly seventy years, which is a record as no other family stayed so many years.

Henry was married in about 1830 to Emma Holdsworth, (I think), with rejoicings no doubt on the joyful occasion. They had four children, but sadly two died when they were babies. Henry's son, Henry Holdsworth Whincup did not follow his father into the Inn-keeping trade, but took up farming and they lived just a couple of miles away at Wittering.

Their younger daughter Frances was born in 1803 and she married John Coverley in the 1830s. John was a farmer at Castle Bytham. We found the two ladies, Frances and Ann, living at 11 Austin Street Stamford on the 1881 census, by now they were both widows. I see on the back of a picture Yvonne has sent me that Ann Chapman died in 1885 aged 85 years.

Their second son Francis was the youngest of the family born in 1813, he took up farming in the nearby village of Ketton, where in September 1837 he married Sarah Lawrance from Dunsby. I believe her family were also farmers.

The family moved in just before Christmas 1815, and Thomas Whincup immediately put a notice in the Mercury stating that he had taken over, and it was business as usual.

Like the previous tenants, besides taking the George Inn and premises, he also leased George farm, Nuns Close, Nun's meadow and the Great Close for a total of £378.00 per year.

Thomas Whincup held an auction on Friday 12th January 1816 at 12 o'clock, he was selling 2 lots of Hogarth Prints. They were Harlot and The Rakes Progress and were sold by Mr Joseph Wright. The prints could be seen at the George, where they had hung ever since they were published in 1734 to 1735 and previously owned by Thomas Alcock or Brian Hodgson who had kept the Inn at that time.

On the 26th January 1816 there was a cock-Fight, most probably in a large room in the courtyard, although there was a purpose built cock-pit it was not always used. This particular fight was for a large prize, the prize being a Fat Ox!

An auction was held at the Inn on Tuesday 1st October 1816 selling fine Books and Prints, also some pieces of Needlework, which were much sort after in those days.

Thomas Whincup offered a reward of 5 Guineas for a Posting Mare, which stood 15 hands high and of a light colour, that was stolen from a close in Wothorpe, January 1817.
A further reward of 10 Guineas was offered by the Stamford and St. Martins Association for the Prosecution of Felons.

In April 1817 this notice appeared in the Stamford Mercury: A Market Ordinary will be provided on Friday the 18th April and continuing every Friday. Dinner will be on the Table at 2.30pm. Thomas was certainly doing all he could to increase business for the George.

Joseph Kilbourn who had been an ostler at the Inn for a number of years, decided to take over the newly erected Anchor Inn, just across the road near to the bridge, (now Pizza Express), this was in January 1821.

An update for coaches in the 1820s: **A typical Mail Coach from the 1820s**

MAIL-COACH BUILT BY WAUDE

The Edinburgh, York, Stamford and London Mail Coach with a guard arrives at the George Inn, Stamford at 7.30pm every evening, then to the Bull and Mouth Inn, London arriving at 6am.
It leaves the Bull and Mouth Inn London at 8pm, to arrive at the George Inn at 6.30am.
The Glasgow, Carlisle, Stamford and London arrives at the George Inn Stamford at 11am then on to London to arrive at 9.30pm. It Leaves London at 9pm, to arrive at the George Inn at 6.30am.
The Regent coach now leaves the George Inn Stamford at 7am, to arrive at the Blue Boar Holborn, London at 7pm.

On Monday the 25th February 1822. The Stamford and St. Martins Association for the Prosecution of Felons held their Annual General Meeting at the Inn at 11 o'clock with a dinner to follow at 3pm. The association had quite a number of members, mainly the trades people of the town, it being in their interest to deter thieves.

The association continued meeting at least once a year, it gradually became a social event and it appears to have finished, at the outbreak of the second world war in 1939.

There was a happy event on the 4th September 1822, when Thomas Milner an ostler at the Inn was married to Frances Leeson, who was also employed there. She was the daughter of Michael Leeson, a Plumber and Glazier of the town living in St. George's Square. The ceremony took place at St. Mary's Church.

The Tax commissioners attended the George on Saturday the 2nd November 1822, between 10am to 3pm, for the Tax collectors to pay the money they had collected. This business would have been transacted in one of the Courtyard rooms.

The Stamford and Rutland Bible Society committee meeting was held at the George in July 1823.

Everyone was asked to assemble at 10am and when all the business had finished there would be an ordinary dinner laid on.

A daily scene at the old hostelry was mine host, Henry Whincup standing at the door of his Inn, dressed in his white corduroy breeches and brown top boots. Waiting to welcome the arrival of the mail coach.

A Post Boy named James Eaton, who was employed by Thomas Whincup as a chaise driver at the George Inn, caused a serious loss by his misconduct in March 1825.

He had driven to Empingham village with two travellers who had come to the George Inn by the Regent coach. On his return journey instead of going straight back to the Inn he came down St. Mary's Hill, turned left into Wharf Road a few yards before entering the river at the old ford, with the intention to wash the horses.

As he crossed over to the other bank the force of the water carried the horses and chaise downstream, together with the post boy. His cries of help were heard when he was opposite Mr Phillips Brewery, (this is where Phillips court now stands).

Mr Phillip's pleasure boat was used to save him: James Eaton was standing on top of the chaise with his head just above water when he was saved. Immediately the chaise and horses sank and were drowned.

On the 24th June 1825 the Officers of the Royal Lincolnshire, Militia were entertained at the George, which they used as their Headquarters, when they had an excellent dinner, with the usual speeches and entertainment afterwards. This one was to celebrate the 10th anniversary of the Battle of Waterloo.

In December 1825 The Duke of St. Alban and his party, Charlotte Beauclerk, Mrs. John Coutts and Miss Coutts, had dinner at the George Inn and stayed there the night. They were up early the next morning, and after breakfast set off for London at 6am.

December 1825:
Here are more coach times. The Norwich coach leaves the Norfolk Hotel at 5.45am, and arrives at the George Inn, in time for the North bound coaches.

The Wellington Post leaves the George every morning at 8am travelling North, then at 10am South to London.

The Regent (four inside, light Post Coach) leaves for London every morning at 6.40am. Then leaves from Holborn, London every morning at 7.30am.

A new coach called The Times:

On Monday 7th May 1827, every morning will leave the George Inn at 8am to arrive at the new Angel and Reindeer in Doncaster at 8pm. Then leave Doncaster at 8am arriving at the George at 8pm.

Passengers and parcels can be booked at the General Coach Office, George Inn, St. Martins Stamford.

Justin Simpson an Antiquarian in the 1800s, mentions that Henry Boor the son of old Joe Boor a well known chimney sweep in the town, was for many years a Booking Clerk at the George "In the Palmy old Coaching Days". Henry would enter all the passenger's names and destinations into a ledger. The passenger having paid half his fare when booking and the remainder when he took his seat, he had to book his seat some days in advance.

ALTERATION of TIME in the GLASGOW ROYAL MAIL.

THE public are respectfully informed that on and after the 5th instant the GLASGOW MAIL (through Leeds) will in future go through Pontefract, Doncaster, and Newark, and will arrive at the GEORGE INN, SAINT MARTIN's, STAMFORD BARON, every Evening at half-past 8, for London: starts from London every Evening at 8, and arrives at the George Inn every Morning at half-past 5.

A New Coach (called the TIMES) will, on and after Monday next the 7th instant, leave the GEORGE INN, and BULL AND SWAN INN, SAINT MARTIN's, every Morning at 8, and arrive at Doncaster at 8 in the Evening: will leave the NEW ANGEL and REIN DEER INNS, DONCASTER, every Morning at 8, and arrive at Stamford at 8 in the Evening.

The following Coaches also start from the George Inn, St. Martin's, Stamford Baron:—

ROYAL MAIL, for Edinburgh, (through York,) every Morning at a quarter before 6, and every Evening for London at half-past 8.

REGENT (4-inside light Post Coach), for London, every Morning at 20 minutes before 7.

The Original NORWICH UNION, for Norwich, every Morning at 7, after the arrival of the Highflyer from York.

The WELLINGTON, to London, every Morning at 10.

☞ Passengers and Parcels booked at the General Coach-office, George Inn, St. Martin's, Stamford Baron. 1st May, 1827.

In January 1828 a Lieutenant Colonel Munro had been visiting Lord Howden of Grimstone near Tadcaster, Yorkshire, and spent Tuesday night at Doncaster. On Wednesday feeling unwell he travelled on The Times Coach to the George at Stamford, arriving in the evening.

His writing desk and some important papers could not be found in the coach and this caused him to become very agitated, so he went to bed. His condition worsened, so much that they sent for Mr Jackson who was an Apothecary, and subsequently Dr Arnold, a Surgeon who lived in St. Martins. They did all they could to revive him, but he died about 9pm.

His writing desk did eventually arrive, after his death. There was a coroners report, death was caused by exhaustion and nervous disability. He was buried in St. Martins churchyard on the 15th January 1828. He came from Inverary Scotland.

There was, what was described as a terrible scene at Stamford's Friday Market on the 18th September 1829. Robert Phillips who was an under ostler employed by Mr Whincup of the George Inn, sold his Wife by Auction on Market Hill, (this was the part of Broad Street at the top of Ironmonger Street), to William Brown who was a Labourer from Oakham. He sold her for 4/-, that's 20pence in today's money! Although this was legal the onlookers were very angry indeed, but they were allowed to leave without being molested.

On the 26th March 1830 there was a small, thin Terrier type dog with long ears and a rather long tail. It was either lost or stolen from the George Inn. It had a chain collar engraved Robert Hammond, Swaffham. Return the dog to the Rev. Richard Lucas for a reward of £5. If kept the person will be prosecuted.

In the Assembly suite of the George Inn on Monday the 26th April 1830, there was a meeting of opposition to the suggested alteration of the Great North Road. As you may well imagine there was a massive turn out to oppose the scheme. It concerned the route of the road from Welwyn to Newark. The new road would go through the towns and villages of, Shefford, Titchmarsh, Blatherwycke, Empingham, Exton, Sewstern and Long Bennington. This route would have meant taking all the trade that the Great North Road brought to the George and all the trades people of the town, especially those connected with catering and coach building.

Thankfully the idea was dropped, like many other by-pass schemes, that is until the one in the 1960s, which has helped to control the traffic hold ups that we all experience now.

On the 8th November 1830 a dark brown mare mistakenly taken from the Inn, and the one which was left behind had similar markings. The mare belonged to Mr Johnson of March, and the person concerned was asked to return the mare as soon as possible or face prosecution.

There was an advertisement in the Mercury on the 30th March 1832: Wanted immediately, a Cook who perfectly understands her business, good wages will be given.
Apply personally to Mr Whincup at the George Inn.

Mr. Whincup was to loose two of his staff tragically within days of each other during July in 1832. On Thursday morning the 19th July the Regent coach came into Stamford from the north and when it arrived at the George they realised a passenger should have been picked up in Red Lions Square. John Blades, who was a porter at the Inn, drove the coach back to the Square for the passenger. Upon returning down St. John's Street the two horses became ungovernable and crashed through a greengrocers window into the shop. One of the horses fell partly into the house, and when it was extricated from the coach was led out at the door.
John Blades was thrown from the coach and was severely injured about the head. It was found that the accident was caused owing to a broken bit on one of the bridles. John Blades after suffering in agony died on the following Monday the 23rd. An inquest was held and a verdict of accidental death was recorded. He was buried in St. Martin's churchyard on Wednesday 25th aged 39 years.

The other tragic event was a suicide: At an inquest held on Tuesday 24th July 1832, by the Coroner of the borough, upon the body of Thomas Taylor a single man aged 22, who was an assistant ostler at the George Inn St. Martins. He had taken a quantity of Laudanum, and went into the meadows where he was found in an insensible state, and upon being removed to the Seven Stars public house in the Sheepmarket, was found to be dead. It seems the unhappy lad had formed an attachment with a female of loose character, whom he offered to marry; he afterwards found that she was already a married woman.
He proposed to leave Stamford if she would accompany him, which she declined; this threw him into an unhappy state of mind and he then took the poison. The verdict recorded was insanity.

On the Monday 13th August 1832, George Grummitt was committed for trial at the next Peterborough Sessions charged with feloniously taking a quantity of apples from Mr Whincup's orchard at the rear of the Inn.

Romance was in the air in 1833, when two of the George's employees decided to get married Mr. J. Cobb who was one of the Waiters was married to Miss S. Hill, who was from Stilton. They were married at St. Martins church on the 6th September 1833.

Later in the month, on Friday 27th September, between 6pm and 8pm there was an auction at the saleroom in the George courtyard, of 4 Houses in Burghley Lane, in the occupation of John Reed, John Gardner, Elizabeth Corbett and Thomas Mack, also 3 stables and a coach house. Freehold. There was also a good house and garden in St. Martins lately in the occupation of Mrs Wingfield.

At Peterborough Court Sessions in October 1833 criminals were dealt with far more severely in those days, as we have often been told. Two brothers, Joseph and James Rosling were found stealing fowls from a hen roost on a farm at Wothorpe. The owner was Mr Whincup of the George at Stamford. They were each sentenced to, seven years transportation!

The November fogs were causing havoc with the coaching trade in 1833. The fog was so dense that the mail coach from London to Edinburgh was extremely delayed, and the Edinburgh to London coach arrived at the George two hours late, after overturning the night before in dense fog. Fortunately there was no exterior damage although the passengers and driver would have suffered cuts and bruising, and it would have been a frightening experience.

On the 16th May 1834 there was another wedding, it was between Thomas Eayrs, a cooper in the town and Millicent Bunday, who was a chambermaid at the George, the couple were married at St. Martins church.

There was a sale of horses at the George Inn on Monday the 1st September 1834 at 1pm, when 14 valuable coach horses in high condition had been taken off the London to Lincoln coaches. They could be seen on the Saturday preceding the day of sale, by applying to the ostler at the Inn.

We can look at Stamford's weather in 1836. January of that year commenced with severe frosts, temperatures were down to 22°f -5°C. February, which was also a leap year started with 5-6 inches of snow, freezing conditions. and more snow throughout the month. All this would have meant the roads would have been in a treacherous condition, making travelling very difficult for coaches and other road traffic. In those days travellers had to wrap up in coats and blankets, even when riding inside, riding outside would have been worse for the driver and passengers. They would have been half buried in straw and at least two top coats.
March was very wet, with snow and hail later in the month. There was rain and snow in April. In May there was a cold north easterly wind, with thunder later in the month.
Then June was dry and very hot, the temperature reaching 81°f in the shade on the 15th. July– hot and dry heavy rain by the middle of the month, then 3¼ inches of rain fell in 5 hours on the 24th. August was fine and pleasant, 74°f on the 3rd then thundery later. September was an unfavourable month for the harvest, it being wet and showery. October was colder, the Aurora Borealis or Northern lights were brilliant on the 11th of the month, then 5 inches of snow fell in about 6 hours on the 29th. In November there was stormy weather and heavy gales, with snow on the 18th and a heavy thunderstorm on the 28th of the month. December started wet and windy, with frosts in the middle of the month. Then it was fine and pleasant until Christmas when a heavy fall of snow from the northeast on Christmas day and Boxing day, rendered all the roads impassable.

The beginning of 1837 was a cold one, with snow making travelling very difficult in January.

The Birthday of Princess Victoria the heiress to the throne, was observed on the 26th May 1837. The Mayor of the town, Mr Weldon sent out invitations to guests on Monday evening inviting them to dinner at the George Inn on Wednesday.
Of course this did not give anyone enough notice, as many had already made alternative arrangements for the event.
However about 36 gents were able to attend, and they had an evening of splendid entertainment. The very liberal landlord, Mr Whincup, provided excellent provisions, enough in fact for over 100 persons.
The town celebrated, just like a Jubilee, many of the shops were closed and their windows were all lit up. In fact, George Baker the chemist at No. 10 St. Mary's Street, had a large star in the window that was lit up with, P V in large letters. The church bells were rung at various times, and the bands played and marched through the streets. Everyone who could, would have been outside as in those days there was no television or radios, this was the one way they could enjoy themselves.

In December 1837, between 1 and 2am on Sunday morning the 19th there was a robbery at the Tap Room of the Inn. Someone broke in and stole some bedroom furniture also 54 yards of Moreen,

(a heavy fabric of wool or wool/cotton) used in furnishings, also a quantity of wallpaper.
A reward of 5 Guineas was offered by Mr Whincup, and a further 5 Guineas by Mr Hopkinson the Treasurer of the Stamford and St. Martins Association for prosecution of felons.

One of Henry Whincup's Posting mares was involved in a nasty accident in the courtyard of the Inn on February 16th 1838, when the High Flyer Coach was changing horses in the yard. One of Henry's valuable posting mares was going to the stables through the yard, when she fell against a wheelbarrow. The handle shaft snapped off and penetrated the horse's flank, towards the hip. The animal plunged and fell, but the horse keeper managed to hold on and take her into the stable. Mr. Phillipson, a Surgeon, I believe, was called and he was able to extract the piece of wood. The animal made a good recovery.

There was another theft at the Inn on the 20th March 1838. A box containing Trousers and other apparel belonging to John Boor, who was the Boots at the Inn was stolen. The trousers were pawned at James Atton's Pawn Shop at 37 Broad Street. By doing this, the police were able to trace the thief who was, George Whyman, a Labourer and charged him with the theft.

By the late 1830s the railways were being built in some parts of the country. Although they had not reached Peterborough and Stamford yet it was possible to get to London by horse and coach then on the train.
One of the first coaches to do the run was called Railway. In May 1838 it ran from the Red Lion Inn, Bargate, Boston, leaving at 5.45am, arriving at the George Inn Stamford at 10am.
It then proceeded to Denbigh Hall, railway station in Northants, arriving for the 5pm train to London. The train arrived at Euston at 7pm. That journey would take 9 hours whereas the mail coach took 10½ hours.
Now we can get from Stamford to London via Peterborough in under 2 hours.

Her Majesty Queen Victoria's Accession to the Throne. A Celebration Dinner.
Henry Whincup gave a very special Dinner on Thursday 28th June 1838, in celebration of Queen Victoria's Coronation. The tickets were One Guinea each, this was for the Dinner and Dessert Wine. The Dinner was to commence at 4pm. This may sound early to sit down for Dinner, but it wasn't until the 1900s when dinner, the main meal of the day was eaten in the evening. Gentlemen wishing to attend the dinner were asked to purchase their tickets at the Bar, on or before the 25th June.

On the 3rd September in that year, Mr Henry Whincup was convicted of Gaming at his Inn.
Mr Whincup had a party of friends that he was entertaining in one of the rooms. A William Chesterton overheard them talking and thought they were gambling. He called the Police and Mr Whincup said they were just playing cards, one guest Mr Harper, who I think was a Brewer in the town, admitted they were playing sixpenny points at whist, which infringed the Inn's licence. Mr Harper very annoyed and thought it was an intrusion by the police and grabbed one of them by the collar.
Mr. Harper pleaded guilty and was fined 5/-, Mr Whincup, was fined 20/- and costs.

There was a meeting in one of the courtyard rooms at the Inn on Friday the 21st September 1838, for the removal of the Corn Market from the front of Browne's Hospital in Broad Street, into the Portico in the High Street. The Portico was built in the early 1800s to house the Meat and Fish markets. The meeting decided in favour of the Portico that would have good attendance from buyers and sellers. The Market would start at 1pm.

In December 1838, Sir George Clerk MP arrived at the George, where he was invited to meet his constituents on Tuesday the 18th at 4pm. 58 people attended the meeting and sat down to a very good meal that the landlord had provided for them. There was a charge of 12/- to cover the price of wine. Mr Phillip was the President of the Red committee, Alderman Mills the Chairman, and Mr Gilchrist, Vice-President.

On the 14th February, a fire broke out in the Exeter Room at the Inn, this was a room into which coach passengers were ushered to wait until the horses had been changed, before continuing their journey.
It was about 3am when the fire was discovered, and had taken such a hold that it took the united efforts of Mr Whincup and his staff a good 1½ hours to bring it under control. Fortunately the room was used frequently, or the consequence could have been far worse. It seems that the fire had been smouldering for some time.
It had originated in an old fireplace in the room, which had been covered up, but there was a connection with the new fireplace. A large quantity of soot had collected and set fire to a long beam, which ran across the front of the fireplace.
The town's fire engines were promptly taken into the Inn yard. The management of the fire plugs, (fire hydrants) were entrusted to an old man named John Cragg. John was a pensioner living in The Burghley Alms Houses nearby, but a delay of half an hour arose because the old man could not find his, *wooden leg!*
If you could imagine being woken up in the middle of winter on a dark night. The only light you had would be a candle, when you managed to light it. Outside was dark too, there were no street lights on through the night in those times, so it must have been a bit of a panic for John and his wife.

In April 1839, Henry Whincup held a sale of 27 of his coach horses. This had come about because the Glasgow and the Edinburgh mail coaches had been taken out of service, the mail now being transported by a rail network that was developing throughout the country. Other long distance passenger coaches were being taken off too.
He also advertised a 3 year old, dark Bay Horse for sale, by Red Gauntlet. A thorough bred Mare, in foal to Magnet, and also a young foal by Red Gauntlet.
He also has a prize Stallion "The Magnet" at Stud. He stands 16 hands high, strong and heavy bone, with good muscular power.
This shows how the Inn keepers were involved in Horse breeding, and farming together with the Hostelry trade.

Lincoln to London. A coach leaves the Saracens Head Inn, Lincoln at 6am daily. Arriving at the George Inn Stamford Midday, then continuing to Blisworth Station Northants at 5pm.
Passengers are then able to continue on the Railway train to Birmingham, arriving at 8pm, or take the London train, which arrives at Euston Station at 8.15pm.
A train returns daily at 7.30am and connects with a coach to arrive in Stamford at 4pm.
This was advertised in May 1839 as the demand for rail travel increased, although the railways were not running in Lincolnshire until 1848.

The Stamford Cricket Club, held a match on Stamford Racecourse at 10.30am on Tuesday 24th September 1839. It was between the married and single members. Then, they had their Annual Dinner at the George at 6pm tickets 10/6d. A magnificent meal followed by some entertainment. William Torkington was the captain and secretary, he was also a solicitor in the town.

In one of the Courtyard rooms, Messrs De La Fosse, dentists of 21 Oxford Street London, sent their Mr Gache who was a peripatetic dentist, (that is a journeyman and teacher of the art of dentistry) once a fortnight to attend to cleaning, scaling, stopping and extractions. They also made false teeth. Mr Gache was available on Thursday's between the hours of 11am and 5pm.

The Simon and St. Jude fair which was held every November, was a farm implement, sheep, pigs, cattle and horse fair. The streets were full of animals, implements and also farm produce. There was mention of cheese prices, Leicester at 6½d to 7d a pound. Stilton at 8d to 9d a pound and onions at 1/6d a peck. I understand that the cheese and onion fair was held in Maiden Lane. So many people came into the town that the George Inn was literally overflowing with guests.

On the 22nd November 1839, in a meeting at the Town Hall. Alderman T. C. Hopkinson suggested that the path from the rear of the George Inn across the Lammas bridge, into town, should be re-surfaced and a light be erected.

The rich pasture land in St. Martins known as Cow Pasture was up for auction again, it belonged to the late John Chapman and was in the tenancy of James Pollard who was a well known butcher in the town. The sale was at 6pm on Thursday 11th June 1840 in the auction room at the George.

The Railway Tally Ho coach ran every day, except Sundays starting on the 28th August 1840. It went from Stamford to Syston, leaving the George at 6.30am travelling through Empingham, Oakham, and Melton Mowbray, arriving at Syston at 11am. The return coach leaving Syston at 2.30pm, and arriving at the George at 7pm.

Passengers were able to get from the George to London in 6 hours in 1840. They had now opened a railway line from Blisworth to Peterborough. The coaches leaving the George Inn every morning at 6am, 9.45am and 3pm conveying the passengers to Sibson for their connection to London. It was also possible to get to Birmingham in 5 hours, to Manchester in 8 hours and Liverpool in 9 hours.

When the Dowager Queen Adelaide visited the town on Monday 8th August in 1842, a very colourful triumphal arch was erected over the roadway at the George Inn for her procession through the town.

This is headed Poor Old Horse! About 14 years ago Mr. Whincup of the George Hotel, Stamford, sold a horse to Mr. Francis of Thurlby. He was a carrier, working between Stamford Bourne and Spalding; when he bought the horse it was about 20 years old, and had formerly won a steeple race. At 22 years it could leap over a five bar gate like a buck. It died suddenly last Saturday and was buried on the Monday. This horse was kindly treated by Mr Francis. Though it travelled with a cart 76 miles a week, making in the last 14 years no less than 55,328 miles.
He certainly got a good mileage out of the horse!

With the continuing growth of the railways throughout the country, Thomas and Henry Whincup must have felt concern for their future as it would be obvious of the damage it would inflict upon the coaching trade. They did take measures to sell posting horses when the mail coaches were taken off the roads and the mail sent by the new railway network.

Now in February 1845 there was talk of a plan to bring the railway through the town on the south side of the river, which they eventually did. They were planning however to make the George Inn and premises the site of a first class station. Whatever were they thinking of. This famous old Coaching Inn, which the generations of the Exeter family had rebuilt, and within the last 75 years extended and re-faced the building, would have been lost forever.
I understand that the Marquis of Exeter just would not entertain this idea at all.

By May of that year the Midland railway company and the Marquis had come to an agreement. The paddock area at the rear of the George Inn, and to the west of the Sun Inn, which was on the corner of Church Street and Wothorpe Road, would be the site for the station. This is where the station still stands today, but it now occupies a smaller site.
Excavation work on the railway was started in the autumn of 1845, and by the beginning of October 1846, four trains a day had commenced running.

With the building of the railway, there were some alterations to the George Hotels entrances. The cobbled entrance on High Street St. Martin's was sealed off to traffic and became the reception area that we know today. A new road had to be built on the north side of the George Hotel for traffic to travel along to the railway station and yard. This road was opened for traffic in the winter of 1849.

An entrance was made on this new road for the coaches to enter the Hotel's courtyard, but this is now part of the dining room, however on the outside you can still see the archway with the words, "George Hotel" written across it.

The present side entrance was built at this time, and it is in this area where the cock-pit had been built. When the sport went out of favour it was used for a number of years as a schoolroom, then it was closed and demolished.

On the west end of the stables, there was built a small bar, known as the George Tap.

The Tap was in a prime position being opposite to the station gates and would have been a welcome sight to the weary traveller wanting to refresh himself, before going home or going about his business in the town. When the new Cattle Market was opened next to the station in 1897, the farmers, drovers and anyone attending the Monday cattle market found it a useful watering hole, there was many a deal being made over a pint in the Tap.

With land being taken for the building of the railway, there was a reduction in the rent to £342.00 per year, in 1847.

The Whincup family suffered losses in 1846 and 1848. Thomas died in the autumn of 1846, then Henry's wife Emma, died and was buried at St. Martins church on the 11th July 1848, and she was only 39 years of age.

Henry and his mother had to continue with the Inn that was undergoing a dramatic change, owing to the increasing number of coach passengers using the New railway for their journeys.

From 1845 to 1848, Henry Whincup's auxiliary mail van was sent to Wansford and Sibson Station to collect the London mail. It was in January 1846 when the two horses were released from the van to go into the stables at Sibson, that they trotted of towards the river. Efforts were made to catch them but they got away and later were feared drowned, Henry was naturally upset at loosing two good horses, but they were seen a day or two later and caught at Elton, to be returned to their owner.

With the decline of the coaching trade, the George became a Hotel. Although the mail and other famous coaches had stopped running, there were still a number of smaller coaches and omnibuses running daily.

Two such runs were, the Amnity coach which left the George travelling to Bennington, Newark and Doncaster every week-day, and the Red Rover went every afternoon from the George to Newark and Nottingham.

Chapman's waggons ran a weekly journey. Leaving the George at 5.15am on a Tuesday morning and ran to Wisbech to connect with the Wisbech Packet boat.

Peter Sharman's cart, which started from St. Leonard's Street, called at the George every Monday at 8am, Tuesday and Thursday at 7am, travelling to Peterborough to set down passengers at the Three Tuns Inn, in Cowgate.

The George started to cater more for the railway passengers who came to the town on business, or visitors wanting to shop and enjoy the town's antiquity. They would be able to travel around locally, as Henry Whincup still ran a posting house with Traps and Gigs etc., for hire. Business people and others would have used this form of transport, as there was no other way of getting around, apart from walking.

In December 1850 Henry Whincup was enjoying a days hunting with the Cottesmore hounds on the Grimsthorpe estate, He set his horse to jump a fence, when its fore feet slipped throwing Henry off. The horse fell and rolled on to him causing severe injuries, it was found that he had four broken ribs and a broken collar bone together with much bruising. Mr Graves and several members of the hunt rendered assistance. He was taken to Corby and after being attended by a surgeon there, he was sent home in a fly. There were numerous enquires at the George after the accident, a lot of his friends being concerned about him.

From a Drawing by HERBERT RAILTON.

Is Henry Whincup one of the two gentlemen dressed in their hunting attire?

In his younger days, Henry was described as a rackety lad, one without real vice but who yet contrives to give an immense deal of trouble to his parents, is that "he be one of Tom Whincup's sore uns." This is an old Lincolnshire saying, however Henry became very popular as was noted for his love of sport in all its branches. On one occasion he laid a bet that he would drive a carriage and four at full gallop. From the top of St. Martins, down the hill, turn sharp left and through the narrow arch in Station Road to the Inn yard. This he did missing the arch masonry by a few inches. (The arch now forms part of the dining room).

A more sensational wager had been made earlier in the century when Mr Milton, a well known character, undertook to ride from Piccadilly to the "George", a distance of over 90 miles, within 5 hours. Leaving London at 8 o'clock on a December morning he reached the George, having ridden 13 horses, at 12.25pm. Thus winning his wager by 35 minutes.

Looking at the census for 1851. We find that Henry Whincup was aged 48 years a Farmer and Innkeeper, employing 25 men, this would have been mainly on his 700 acres of farmland. His daughter Emily was living with him, she was aged 19 years, also his mother Sarah Whincup, who like Henry was widowed. In the 1850s Sarah moved back to her native Yorkshire where she died in1865, at the age of 85 years.

There were 8 house servants living in, all of them unmarried –

Jane	Wade	age 40		born Folkingham
Mary	Elliott	" 45	"	Thorney, Northants
Elizabeth	Miller	" 28	"	Deene, "
Olive	Warby	" 17	"	Barnack "

Jane	Mardell	"	25	"	Uffington
Janet	Trowell	"	19	"	Empingham, Rutland
William	Louth	"	20	"	Wansford, Northants
Charles	Bland	"	15	"	Greatford
William	Bellamy	"	40 farm labourer		Stamford

Just 2 visitors staying there:
Mary A. Pawlett aged 19, a farmers daughter from Rippingale.
The other visitor was a Mr Plumer-Roper, he was 23 and a commercial traveller from London.

The 1851 census shows, John Boor and his wife Elizabeth, both Stamfordians, were running the Hotel Tap. John was also employed at the Inn and it was he who had his trousers and other clothes stolen in the 1838, when he was employed as the Boots.

The Marquis of Salisbury had his headquarters at the George during the election in1853, when as Lord Robert Cecil, he was returned, and given a start in active political life, as one of the representatives of the Borough of Stamford, in the House of Commons.

After holding nearly every public office that can be held in a Provincial town, Henry Whincup was elected Mayor in 1853. The Mayor's Banquet being held in the Banqueting Hall at the George.

James Torkington, a prominent solicitor in the town presided over a large public meeting at the George on July 23rd 1857. They had assembled to consider the erection of a new Corn Exchange. After a lengthy discussion, a motion recommending that the site of the Black Swan in Broad Street for the site of the corn market.

At the George Inn on the 1861 Census, Henry Whincup, now aged 58 years, had married again, his second wife was Emma Lawrence, the widow of Thomas Lawrence, a farmer of Hacconby. Their young daughter Sarah aged 4 was living with them.

There was a staff of eight living in -

Miss	Adcock	age 20		Housekeeper	Higham Ferrers	NTH
Ann. M	Batty	"	38	Chambermaid	Swanton Morley	Norfolk
Emma	Palmer	"	24	Cook	Apethorpe	NTH
Jane	Glover	"	22	Housemaid	Market Deeping	
Sarah. A	Huff.	"	18	Barmaid	Wittering	NTH
Sophia	Brewster	"	18	Kitchen Maid	Yarwell	NTH
Jane	Wells	"	17	Nursemaid	Pilsgate	NTH
Abraham	Riley	"	13	Under Waiter	Stamford	

They had two visitors

John. S	Chapman	age 29	nephew	Farmer	Horninghold	Leics.
Louise	Chapman	"	22 niece	Stanground	Hunts.	

In 1861, Thomas Arnold who was from St. Neots, and his wife Sarah were at the Hotel Tap with their children, Mary who was a Straw Bonnet maker and Emma, who was a Dressmaker. Their son Thomas was a Messenger in the Telegraph office at the Great Northern railway station.

There was a series of St. Martins Penny Readings in the ttown, these were religious talks and were given by The Rev. C.J. Dyer in 1865. He used various venues and on February 10th he gave his third in the Banqueting room at the George, this was one of the suite of rooms in the south wing. It was an evening of talks, also music and singing, making it a very enjoyable evenings entertainment. People were very restricted for entertainment in those days radio, and the cinema had not been invented then. All the proceeds went to the St. Martins soup kitchens, to help to feed the poor through the cold winters.

On the 21st February 1865, Charles White a coachman died at Liverpool, he was aged 65. Charles was a very well known coachman, driving The Times coach between Stamford and Doncaster. He was one of the most celebrated Whips on the Great North Road. When the railway came to Stamford he drove Henry Whincup's horse drawn Omnibus to the Station, to meet the Hotel passengers arriving and to take those travelling by train.

The Stamford Races in 1865, were very successful according to Mr Merry who was Clerk of the course. On the Monday evening of race week at the George, the stands and booths were let by auction. The races commenced on the Thursday, and all the trains coming into the town were crowded with race officials and the general public attending the races. The George hotel was fully booked all of the week, and the bars and restaurant were inundated with customers.

The Freemasons of The Lodge of Merit No. 466 held their first meeting on the 16th June 1865 at 3pm, in one of the Assembly Rooms on the south side of the courtyard at the George. Many of the town's tradesmen and professional people were becoming members, after the meeting they all sat down to a magnificent banquet provided by Brother Whincup.

It was in 1881 that the Prince and Princess of Wales, who were guests at Burghley, visited Stamford and were presented with an address by the Freemasons, who were gathered outside at the front of the George Hotel. The Prince later became King Edward VII.
Regular meetings were held here until 1925.
When the rooms in the courtyard were being redecorated in November 1984, underneath five layers of wallpaper were found a wall that featured Masonic symbols. Masonic decorations were also on the ceiling and corners of the room. Murals such as this, with a well known design featuring an assemblage of Masonic symbols are not uncommon, but the one at the George was unusually large.

The fine Banqueting Hall at the George was used on October the 6th 1865 to celebrate the Annual Municipal Banquet given by the Mayor Mr J. Groves. The Borough members of Parliament, Viscount Cranborne, Sir Stafford Henry Northcote, and the Corporation attended.

The George Hotel was fully booked on Stamford Race Week again in July 1866.
The meeting on the 19th to 20th July was the most successful ever known. On the Stamford Cup value 100 sovereigns, there was very heavy betting. Lord Cardigan's Tormentor (the winner of the Oaks) and Mr Sutton's Elland being pitted against each other for heaps of money. Lord Cardigan's horse Tormentor was the winner. The admissions totalled £500.00 for the two days racing and this was just for the white stand.

The Thirtieth Anniversary of the Loyal Albion Lodge of Odd Fellows, was held at the Banqueting Hall of the George Hotel, on Monday 7th September 1868.
Dinner would be on the table at 3 o'clock precisely. The Right Hon. Sir J.C.D Hay Bart. MP, had kindly consented to take the chair, and was supported by W.U. Heygate Esq. MP.
His worship the Mayor J. Clapton Esq. and the Magistrates, Corporation and Gentlemen of the town and neighbourhood were also present.
During dinner the band played a selection of Quadrilles, Waltzes, Gallops, and Polkas, Henry Whincup had served an excellent dinner, which was followed by 19 toasts and, I expect nearly as many speeches.
The evening's entertainment was by Mr Thaddeus Wells quadrille band, four vocalists, and also two pianos. The vocal and instrumental arrangement were conducted by Thaddeus Wells and also Mr A. Martin of Leicester, with Mr Charles Pearce presiding at the pianoforte. Thaddeus

was a very well known professor and teacher of music in the town, he was also the Organist at St. Michael's church in the High Street.

The Hotel's fine Banqueting Hall was in use again in October 1869, when Garmston Chapman who was the Mayor of the town, held the Annual Municipal banquet there.
Garmston was a well known and respected Draper who ran his well established business in the High Street.

Along Station Road at the rear of the George, the George Tap in 1871 was being run by a locally born lady, Sarah Arnold a widow aged 58 years, and her unmarried daughter, Mary Ann aged 26 years, who was a Barmaid.

Looking at the 1871 census for the George Hotel, Henry Whincup is 68 years old, and living with him is his wife Emma aged 38 and their young son, David who is aged 6 yrs.

There were nine members of the staff who were living in -

Mary	Sharpe	age.43	Housekeeper	Witham-on-the-Hill
Ellen	Close	" 34	Cook	Algarkirk
Mary	Askam	" 23	Chambermaid	Peterborough
Mary	Agar	" 24	Housemaid	Hanningfield ESS
Mary	Wann	" 24	Housemaid	Baston
Mary	King	" 25	General servant	Southorpe
William	Bradford	" 23	Porter	Morton
Henry	Harrold	" 21	Waiter	Ashdon ESS
George	Hand	" 17	Groom	Easton-on-the-Hill

The Stamford Race week, on July 25 to 26th 1873, was to be the last meeting as over the last few years attendances had dropped dramatically. This was the last time the George would be the host for the Judges, Officials and race goers.
The Burghley Handicap, was won by Mr O.L. Evans, horse Sybarite, who was ridden by Mr Luke. At this meeting Fred Archer rode to victory on Mr C.S. Hardy's horse Peacock, in the Borough Members handicap of 5 Sovereigns each and 50 added.

There was rejoicing in the town on September 7th 1875, when Henry, the 4th Marquis of Exeter, and his bride Isabella Whichcote travelled through the town on their way to Burghley House from Aswarby, where they had been married. They were escorted by 200 of the Burghley tenants and the route through Stamford was splendidly decorated and all the church bells were ringing. At the George over 100 Burghley tenants and others sat down to a meal and entertainments, under the presidency of Mr James Sanderson, who was steward to the Marquis of Exeter.

A very sad incident happened at the George in March 1876, when John Robert Bryan who was a farmer and grazier at Bringhurst in Leicestershire committed suicide whilst staying one night at the hotel. It would appear that he had come to Stamford to see the Marquis of Exeter's steward, as he had been discharged from both of his farms which he leased from the Burghley estate, but had got himself into financial difficulty.
William Dennis, a waiter at the hotel said that Mr Bryan arrived about 11am on the Thursday morning and had a soda and brandy. He went out and then came back at 1pm, when he had a bowl of soup and a glass of sherry. In the afternoon he called at Mr Patterson the chemist's, and asked for a pint of laudanum, which he said he wanted for lambing purposes. Joseph Stanford, the assistant sold it to him, but was not suspicious, as he knew Mr Bryan had purchased laudanum on previous occasions for this purpose.

He had dinner at the George at six o'clock in the evening with a pint of sherry and a glass of old ale. During the evening he drank two more glasses of soda and brandy, retiring for bed at ten thirty with a glass of brandy taken up to his bedroom.

In the morning at about 7am he rang his bell for a glass of neat brandy, which the boots boy William Murray took to him. He asked to be called at 11am, but when aroused he said he would be up in a few minutes, at about 11.30am the boots and the waiter went to his room but could not rouse him and sent for a doctor and Mr Whincup, also the housekeeper, Miss Fox. They saw on the wash table a bottle labelled laudanum and a revolver. Dr. Newman arrived just after 12 o'clock and found him lying on his side in agony, having difficulty breathing he tried to revive him but John Bryan died at about 12.45pm.

The jury unhesitatingly recorded a verdict of, Temporary Insanity.

At the beginning of 1879 Henry Whincup decided to retire from the George Hotel.

It was in December 1815 that his father Thomas Thompson Whincup took over the business, he continued building up this old established and first class coaching inn, with the help of his son Henry. In the 1840s Henry took over when his father died. Now 64 years later it had become a first class world wide renowned hotel.

In April 1879 another farmer was to take over the lease of the George, he was Robert Kirkman. Robert was born in 1815 at Garlands Lane Farm, Barlestone, Leicestershire, where he grew up and took up farming like his father before him.

Eventually he moved to Little Oxendon in Northamptonshire where he farmed until about 1877. His first wife died in 1875 and in 1887 he married his second wife, Julia Ann Kebble at Tonbridge, Kent. Julia was 35 years younger than Robert and may have been a barmaid at the Bull and Swan in St. Martins, as her father Thomas Kebble was the landlord in the late 1870s.

He took over the George Hotel and premises, with the farm and land at Wothorpe and Easton for a rental of £480 per year.

Robert Kirkman on his rounds, a more environmental way of travelling around his farm.

At his hotel Robert entertained his friends royally, and was himself a three bottles of Port a day man, also a famous trencherman. That was someone who ate heartily and enjoyed his food.

In the days before central heating, bedrooms were cold places to sleep, so Robert slept in a huge four-poster bed. Rumour had it that his two comely, buxom and personal maids, Susan and Helen, slept on either side of him, keeping him warm and comfortable. There were no electric blankets in those days!

St. Swithin's day in 1880 was a day to remember in Stamford. In the morning there was a terrible thunderstorm followed by torrential rain, which caused the river Welland to rise and overflow into the surrounding streets. Soon scores of men were seen carrying goods, women and children to safety. The Town Hall immediately opened its doors to accommodate them, as did the George Hotel, making its uppers floors available, as the flood waters reached nearly to the top of the pockets of the Billiard table. It covered the spacious courtyard to a depth of several feet, and floated casks of wine and spirits, and ale in a very ungentle fashion. Disconnecting three of them from the beer engine in the bar. The water along Water Street was said to be six feet deep.

On the 1881 census we find that Robert Kirkman was aged 65, and he employed 6 men and 3 boys on his 350 acre farm. His wife Julia was born in Daventry, Northants. She was aged 30. There is no mention of any children, but a list of staff living in -

Isabella	Buevis	age 20	Housemaid	born	Moulton Marsh
Elizabeth	Midgley	" 28	Housekeeper	"	St. Martins Stamford
Alfred	Marshall	" 18	Under waiter	"	Hinckley, Leics.
John T.	Boughton	" 26	Boots	"	St. Martins Stamford
Mary A.	Arden	" 26	Kitchen maid	"	Ryhall, Rutland
Emma A.	Freeman	" 21	Housemaid	"	Ketton "
George	Shearing	" 19	Groom	"	Shelford, Cambs

One Lodger: A guest perhaps, John Archibald Tryon aged 20, he was born in Bermuda in the West Indies, his occupation being, 2nd Lieutenant, Northampton and Rutland Militia, and a Student of Corpus Christi College, Cambridge.

Henry Whincup and his wife Emma were living at No.1 Church Street, just up the road from the George Hotel, having retired two years previously. This was recorded in the 1881 census, but sadly he died on the 8th of July in 1881, at the age of 78 years.

On the 1881 census at the George Tap in Station Road, Charles Murray and his wife Mary ran the Inn. Charles was also employed as a groom and ostler at the Hotel, and Mary was a housekeeper there.

The George was to change hands again in 1881. From Lady Day, Andrew John Moyes leased the hotel premises, gardens and also land at Easton. He was born in Cambridge and was the son of Andrew H. Moyes, who was a hotel keeper in the city of Cambridge.

The Hotel was used as the Conservative Headquarters in the elections of 1882. When, on March 3rd, Mr Morgan Howard QC. addressed a meeting in the Banqueting room, and he was adopted as Conservative member for Stamford.

A Lacrosse match in Burghley Park attracted a very large number of people on Saturday 19th September in 1885. Lacrosse was a ball game that had been invented by the American Indians, and it was a novelty in this part of the country. The game was played between the Gentlemen of Nottinghamshire and Derbyshire. Nottingham county won by 5 goals to 4.

The outcome of this was a meeting held at the George Hotel with a view to forming a Stamford and District Lacrosse club. This took place on Monday the 12th October 1885, when Mr Bromley of North Luffenham Hall presided. The Marquis of Exeter was asked to become President and the Earl of Rosslyn Vice President. On the night of the meeting 25 members enrolled. If all parties would give their consent, the cricket ground in Burghley Park would be used for lacrosse, and the new club called, The Burghley Park Lacrosse Club.
Several of the Nottingham players agreed to assist in the games.

In 1885, on the 5th December Mr W. T. Marriott QC. MP. for Brighton, and Colonel Duncan who was MP. for the Holborn division, spoke at a public meeting which was held in the assembly room of the George Hotel, in support of the candidature of Lord Burghley. The polling was for a seat in North Northamptonshire, which included St. Martins Stamford Baron. The polling took place on the 8th December and Lord Burghley was duly elected.

The Assembly room in the George courtyard was very busy on Wednesday February 8th 1888, when the Marquis of Exeter offered 31 lots of property in the town for auction.

They consisted of family residences, cottages, yards and eligible building sites:

There were houses at No. 10 Broad Street, No.3 Wharf Road, No's. 61, 62, and 63 St. Leonard's Street, No's. 6, 9 and 10 North Street. A shop in Red Lion Street, No.1 Ironmonger Street and No's. 68 and 69 High Street. Quite a number of building plots too were up for auction in the following roads, Tinwell Road, Empingham Road, Casterton Road, Recreation Ground Road, and plots in what is now Stanley Street and Vine Street. Two large yards, one in North Street and another one in West Street.

BOROUGH OF STAMFORD,
LINCOLNSHIRE.

TO INVESTORS, BUILDING SOCIETIES, BUILDERS, AND OTHERS.

Particulars and Plans with Conditions of Sale
OF VALUABLE FREEHOLD

BUSINESS PREMISES,
FAMILY RESIDENCES,
COTTAGES, YARDS,
AND SEVERAL
ELIGIBLE BUILDING SITES,
In various Parts of the Borough,

Which will be offered for Sale by Auction,
IN 31 LOTS, BY

MESSRS. RICHARDSON,

AT THE "GEORGE" HOTEL, STAMFORD,
ON WEDNESDAY, FEBRUARY THE 8TH, 1888,
At FOUR for FIVE o'clock in the Afternoon.

Particulars and Plans with Conditions of Sale can be had, and further information obtained at the Offices of the AUCTIONEERS, in Stamford; or of
Mr. CHARLES THORPE, Land Agent, Burghley Offices, Stamford.
Messrs. WALFORDS, Solicitors, 27, Bolton Street, Piccadilly, London, W.

Howard, Printer, Stamford

On Lady Day (March 25th) 1888, Andrew John Moyes and his wife Annie decided to leave the George and moved into the Stamford Hotel in St. Mary's Street.

The George was then leased to Mr F.M. Chapman, who in September 1888 took over the hotel and premises, yard, garden and paddock at a rental of £150.00 per year.
Part of the premises, the Blacksmith's forge was let to Alfred Pearson at £10.00 per year.
He lived at No. 2 St. Mary's Hill with his family.

After the retirement of Henry Whincup, whose name was famous in the coaching era, the George, that used to be one of the best houses on the Great North Road started to fall into decay. The Plate and Furniture had to be sold. As it still had splendid capabilities, it was closed in 1889 for essential structual alterations.

The building on the West side of the courtyard consisted of three stables, each one was divided into three, they were built in the 1780s by Thomas Manton, a local Stone mason. With the decline of the coaching trade during the latter part of the 1800s, and the use of fewer horses these stables were not used, and the northern part was eventually used as garages.
It was at this time that the first floor of the building was converted into a superb Ballroom, and was complete with a minstrel's gallery. This gave the couples more room for dancing.
It was also known as the Long Room and was available for parties and balls etc. being in use into the early 1900s. The orchestra providing music for, The Polka, Gavotes, Military Two Steps, Waltzes, and all the latest dances, with the couples dancing the night away. It has now been converted into bedrooms, but above the ceiling the minstrel's gallery still remains.

On the 29th October 1890 the newly formed Burghley Park Golf Club, held their inaugural meeting at the George Hotel. After over 100 years it is still providing excellent facilities for it's members and visitors.

By 1891 the George was open again for business.

The census shows that, Elizabeth Dawkins a single lady age 36 was manageress of the Hotel, she came from Broughton in Northants. Living at the hotel was Emily Millie Wallace, she was employed as a Bookeeper. Millie age 23 was from Mayfair in London.

There were four domestic staff living in -

Sarah C.	Porter,	age 26	born	East Halton, Nothants
Madeline	Richards	" 36	"	Kettering, "
Maria	Leach	" 26	"	Caultby, Yorks
Edward	Woods	" 21	"	Stamford

In the 1890s the George was advertised as being near to the Polo, Golf and Cricket grounds in Burghley Park. There was also a horse drawn omnibus available to take Hotel guests to visit the State Rooms of Burghley House.

With some of the stables in Station Road being surplus to the Hotel's requirements. George Miles, who had saw mills in the Station yard, took a sub lease on these in 1897 at £6.00 per year. It was also in 1897 that the George paddock was acquired by the borough to build the cattle market, for centuries it had been used as a farmstead in the tenancy of the landlord.

A quiet moment in the courtyard

This tranquil scene was taken about 1900, when William King was landlord of the hotel.
In the left hand corner was the entrance from Station Road, still used by horse drawn vehicles, mostly local traffic now as the motor car, or the horseless carriage, as it was called was beginning to appear on the roads.

The 20th century brought a lot of changes to the hotel trade. It saw the end of the coaching era, and the beginning of the motor car.

The RAC, which was called the Automobile Club when it was formed in 1897, had in the touring section of their handbook, a list of officially appointed hotels and repairers.
The George was first mentioned in 1905, so this must mean that in 2005 it celebrates 100 years of RAC approval.
The entry reads, "The hotel is 92 miles from London, BBB (Bed, Bath and Breakfast) 6 shillings. Car storage for one day and night is free. No charge for a parked car, while the occupants are partaking of meals and refreshments."

It was in 1907 when King Edward VII bestowed the royal title on it, to become the Royal Automobile Club.
In the early days of motoring petrol was not readily available, so a number of the Hotels seized on this opportunity by selling petrol in two gallon cans.

After years of communicating by letter and then by telegrams, there was this new invention the telephone. Many people were reluctant to use the telephone, it was regarded as a gimmick, but the Hotels were quick to realise it's potential and the George became one of the first to use this new invention. Their first number was Stamford 301, and there would only have been one telephone in the reception, whereas today a telephone is available in every guest room. All departments are able to communicate with each other this way and now the mobile phone.

The advent of electricity at the beginning of the century has been a major asset too, enabling the use of electricity for food preparation and cleaning. Then of course lighting by electric power, which is much safer than the gas and earlier days of paraffin and candles.

In the early 1900s it was still very hard work for the housemaids and chambermaids. Carpets were available in squares, which meant polishing and dusting the sides of the room floors. Plumbing was also basic, before en-suite bedrooms, the chambermaid would have taken hot water up to the guest rooms. The guests using a jug and basin, which stood on a wash stand in the room. When retiring at night, a small cupboard next to the bed contained a chamber pot, which the chambermaid discreetly emptied with the washing water into a slop pail the next morning.
I was told that one gentleman, would leave a tip for the chambermaid of one guinea, which had been placed in the chamber pot!

The hotel was to change hands again in 1900, when William King who came from Lutterworth in Leicestershire. He took the hotel premises, yard and garden on a 14 year lease, at a yearly rental of £130.00 for the first seven years. William and his wife Mary Ann took possession in July of that year.

The next year, on the 1901 census we see that William King was 47, and his wife, Mary Ann was 54 and she was born in Liverpool Road London. Their Stepson, Frederick H. Welch living with them, age 27, single and an ostler from Dover.

There were seven staff living in -

Kathleen	Linford	age27	who was the hotel manageress – she came from Kings Lynn	
Nina C.	Smith	" 26	Barmaid	Bourton, Gloucs
Hanna	Oldham	" 26	Barmaid	Newborough, Northants
Fanny C.	Richard	" 25	Chambermaid	Tansor, Northants
Ellen	Groom	" 25	Waitress	Eye, Suffolk
Annie	Burton	" 20	Kitchen Maid	Barnack, Northants
John Wm.	Chapman	" 28	Boots	Ruskington, Lincs

A Retired Hotel proprietor and his wife, Walter S. and Henrietta A. Harr, were guests.
Walter had kept the Crown Hotel in All Saints Place, but now he was retired he ran the Livery Stables, with Broughams, Landaus, Brakes and Waggonettes. With four in hand team and four horse ride and drive team. They catered for Weddings, and also for Funerals.

In 1901 Clarence Scholes was an ostler and groom at the George Hotel, and his wife Roseanne kept the Hotel Tap.

The Stamford Angling Association held their Annual General Meeting in the assembly room of the George Hotel on the 1st March 1901. Mr George Bacon, a Plumber and a devoted follower of the sport, chaired the meeting. He reported that the total number of members was 73, there being 16 new members in the past year. The Angling association made the George their venue for meetings for many years.

It was at the end of March in1901 when some of the tenant farmers on the Burghley estate met at the George. They had assembled to select a present for the Marquis of Exeter's marriage to the Hon Myra Orde-Powess in April. The gift chosen was a large round silver gilt tray, which would be inscribed with the Burghley Coat of Arms in the centre. Mr L. Fortescue presided over the meeting, and Mr P.H. Close, the Hon. Sec. was also present.

The couple were married on Tuesday 16th April 1901 at Wensley church nr. Bedale, then travelling by train to Essendine. The mounted tenants and friends who wished to join in the procession were requested to meet at the George Hotel at 4.30 pm. They proceeded from the George towards Essendine to meet the couple, who where already on their way to Stamford in the State carriage with four horses and Postillion. The couple received a tumultuous welcome as the procession moved through the town and up to Burghley House.

At night the Marquis entertained about 500 guests in the town, some at the George Hotel, some at the assembly rooms, and other hotels in the town.

The annual general meeting of the Stamford Habitation of the Primrose league was held in the assembly room of the George in July 1901, when Mr H. Wing presided over a moderate attendance. An excellent speech was made during the evening by Lord Willoughby De Eresby, MP. and the Marquis of Exeter was present. It was reported that the usual ball held in January, although not so well attended, was very enjoyable and financially successful.

The Primrose league was founded in the 1880s by Benjamin Disraeli and Lord Randolph Churchill, to promote the principles of Tory democracy to all classes of people.

In April 1906 John Gaudern Lovell was an ostler at the George Hotel and also manager of the George Tap, a position he had held from 1903.

He was accused of stealing two fowl the property of Harry Samuel Singleton of the Millstone Inn. The fowl were kept in a field opposite the Bottle Lodges on the Wothorpe Road and the value was 6/6d. He said he thought they were the ones lost by a Mr John Hollis, who was the Bailiff for Lord Cecil. One of the grooms at the Hotel was Harry Kirby who had to give evidence, and another was Arthur Hippy he was also a groom there. Upon the evidence the court decided that John Lovell was not guilty of the theft.

William King managed the George until 1906, when Messrs C.A. Whittingham, R.H. Tebb and R. Aden, took the hotel and premises, on a lease of £150 for the next 10 years.

Miss Selina Mary Stevens, who with her sister Ann, became resident directors and ran the hotel throughout the first world war until about October 1918.

John Godfrey and Co. Ltd, the Timber, Corn and Coal Merchants, whose business was at the rear of the hotel, held their Annual General Meeting and dinner in the banqueting room of the George in November 1906. After the discussion of a good business year they enjoyed an entertaining evening.

Christmas has always been a busy time at the George. On December 20th 1906, a smoking concert was organised by the Northamptonshire Conservative and Unionist Association.

A capital musical programme had been arranged by the committee, together with a large variety of refreshments. The Chairman was J.H.T Phillips as the Marquis of Exeter was indisposed. The meeting was addressed by, T. Ablewhite, conservative agent for Stamford, and H.G Varah, agent for North Northants.

For many years the George has had links with the local Military associations. It was in November 1911 that the D. company of the 4th Battalion Lincs., Regiment held their 52nd Annual dinner in the Banqueting room. Capt. L.H.P. Hart presided over nearly 90 members. As usual the Hotel provided a first class dinner, and during the repast the band of the corps, under the direction of the bandmaster J. Ambler played selections of music in the courtyard.

The loyal toasts having been honoured, the Mayor, Mr James Dalton distributed the prizes won in the recent shooting competition. Then followed a number of speeches and musical entertainment to finish off the occasion.

In the summer of 1912 the hotel courtyard resembled a scene from Tudor times. The Mayor Mr J.B. Corby and members of the corporation had assembled, resplendent in their Tudor costumes complete with ruffs around their necks. They were to ride on horseback through the streets of the town to the Infirmary grounds.

The Infirmary fete was held every year to raise funds and it drew crowds of people to the town, to watch the procession and enjoy the entertainment.

The special pageant this year was to commemorate 350 years since queen Elizabeth I visited the town and was entertained in lavish style by her Senior Statesman Sir William Cecil, the first Lord Burghley.

On behalf of Miss Stevens of the George Hotel, Mr R.S. Cox made an application for the extension of the licence until 2 o'clock on the Saturday morning on the occasion of a Ball being held there on Friday 24th January 1913. The magistrate granted the request. Superintendent Theaker suggested that if possible the house should be closed so far as the public is concerned, at 11pm. The other houses would be closed at 11pm, and it would not be right if people leaving these other houses could go to the George to purchase drink up to 2am on Saturday morning. The licence ought of course, to be confined to those attending the Dance. It was understood that this would be the case.

The Ball was organised by the Northamptonshire Conservative and Unionist association, and it was held in the Long Room, which Miss Stevens had decorated very tastefully for the occasion. The music for the ball was provided by Mr W. Moore and his orchestra.

The Marchioness of Exeter attended along with Sir Arthur and Lady Capelle Brooke, J.H.T Phillips, Miss Gladys Phillips and Miss Phillips, Major and Mrs Pinder and others.

Would You Like a Better Life, in one of our Commonwealth Countries?

Mr E.B Harford an agent for the Canadian Pacific Railways, advertised that he would be at the George Hotel every Monday from March 1913. As someone who had worked on the Prairies, he would be able to give information and advice to anyone interested in settling in Canada. Ontario urgently needed Farmers and Farm hands, good wages could be earned on the land and also good prospects for Domestic servants.

The local lodge of Freemasons held their annual installation festival at the George in September 1914. After the installation and other business was finished, the customary banquet was dispensed with owing to the outbreak of the war. The members instead made a handsome contribution to the War Relief distress fund.

During the early part of World War One, Ann Stevens one of the directors of the George Hotel became a Lady Volunteer Worker, along with other ladies in the town, to help with various war projects such as knitting socks, gloves and balaclavas and sending food parcels.

In 1916 the rent was increased to £160.00 per year and at Michaelmas, the remainder of the lease was transferred to The George Hotel Stamford Ltd. This was in the partnership of Mr George Harry Willis and Mr Sidney Jones.

On April 12th 1918 the Stamford Angling Association held their annual General Meeting at the George Mr G.H. Burton was the Chairman and Mr H.N Fisher, a Hairdresser and Fishing tackle stockist in the High Street, was the Treasurer. After the business was conducted they had refreshments and entertainment.

In December 1918 there was a theft. Emily Ulyett a domestic servant was accused of stealing a blanket, valued at 18/- earlier in the month. Miss Pitt, the resident director of the hotel recognised the blanket as belonging to the George. Emily was remanded in custody until the next week, but we have been unable to read the court case so we don't know what her sentence was.

At the end of the First World War in 1918, Dorcy Mabel Pitt became the Resident Director of the George Hotel. She was a lady from the West country, being born at Canon Frome near Hereford in the 1880s, her father Walter Pitt, was a Farmer and had been a coach maker in earlier years. She was to continue at the George until about 1941.

In 1924. A famous English Film Star of that era, Mr Henry Edwards, who was motoring through Stamford on Wednesday the 30th April with a party of friends called at the George Hotel to have Breakfast and refresh themselves. Henry Edwards was born at Weston Super Mare September 18th 1882, and was on the stage from 1900, he then took Gentlemanly romantic leads in films in the 1920s. Later he directed films and came back to acting as an amiable elderly man. He married the Actress Crissie White in 1922, and died in 1952 at the age of 70 years.

In the early 1900s the George was extended and included The Hermitage, a house next door to the hotel in St. Martins. Then in the 1920s, during George Willis's occupation considerable alterations took place in the hotel.

On the ground floor, the Winter Garden on the east wing was altered together with toilet facilities, and the north wing, the entrance to the courtyard was sealed off and extensions were made to the dining room and the kitchens were re-modelled.

On the first floor the south and west wing had two new bathrooms and additional bedrooms, bringing the total of bedrooms to 57. In those days none of them were en-suite

The Architects involved in the alterations were Traylen and Lenton, who were a well known local firm.

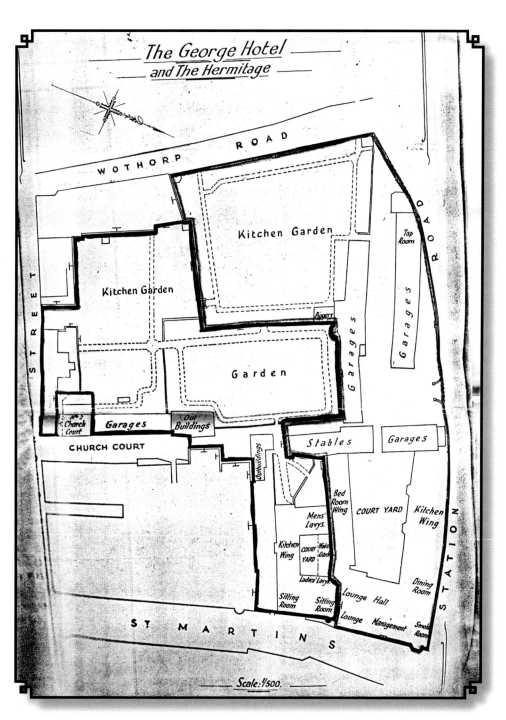

It was in 1924 that the Marquis of Exeter sold the franchise of the George Hotel to Mr George Harry Willis and Mr Sidney Jones, on a 60 year lease for £25,500.

We did some research on the two gentlemen and found that Albert Sidney Jones was a well known and respected Dental surgeon, who had his practice at 59-60 High Street St. Martins, literally just up the road from the George and he was born in the town.

George Harry Willis was a Solicitor, in the practice of Willis and Willis of 59 Chancery Lane, in the City of London, they also had an office in Barnes. He was born at New Malden in Surrey during the 1860s. George lived with his wife, Clara Caroline and their daughter, Doris, in Kingston-upon-Thames, travelling between his solicitors practice in London and his other business interest, the George at Stamford. During his absence Dorcy Pitt continued to run the hotel very efficiently. It was in October 1937 that George lost his wife Clara, she was buried at Kingston-upon-Thames.

No.	When Married	Name and Surname	Age	Condition	Rank or Profession	Residence at the time of Marriage	Father's Name and Surname	Rank or Profession of Father
100	October 24 1938	George Harry Willis	73	Widower	Solicitor	New Malden with Coombs, Surrey	Harry Willis	Dressmaster Coachbuilder & Farmer
		Dorcy Mabel Pitt	56	Spinster	—	Winterbourne Gunner	Walter Pitt	

1938. Marriage solemnized at the Parish Church in the Parish of Winterbourne Gunner in the County of Wilts

Married in the Parish Church according to the Rites and Ceremonies of the Established Church by licence or after _____ by me,
This Marriage was solemnized between us, { George Harry Willis / Dorcy Mabel Pitt } in the Presence of us, { Doris Willis / Hadley John Pitt } Frank Elcho Skynner Rector

We have found that in October 1938 he was married to Dorcy Mabel Pitt, this came to light quite by chance. We were looking through the voters lists for 1937 to 1939 and found, that at the George in 1937 there was Dorcy Mabel Pitt, but in 1939 it was Dorcy Mabel Willis, so we searched for and found their marriage certificate. They were married at Winterbourne Gunner in Wiltshire, it looks as though Dorcy's family had moved into Wiltshire.

On the marriage certificate George was 73 years of age and Dorcy 56 years of age. One of the witnesses was Doris Willis, who I imagine was George's daughter, the other was Hadley John Pitt, who may have been Dorcy's brother.

Stamford was, "On The Air", in February 1935. The BBC's Microphone at Large series, were presenting the town to the world from a travellers point of view. Mr Reed, a nephew of Dame Sybil Thorndike, was telling the story of the Great North Road past, present and future. For this purpose he would introduce an old coaching scene at the George Hotel, then follow this up with the modern motor coach, and to give a glimpse into the future, transport in the air.

Dorcy Willis continued running the George until 1941 when Miss Alice Mary Ann Taylor took over the management of the hotel.

I am not sure when, but George and Dorcy eventually moved to Birdlip, a small town near Cheltenham. It was here that George died in April 1946 at the age of 81 years. Dorcy lived another five years, she died in the Imperial Nursing Home at Cheltenham in December 1951, aged 69 years.

With the outbreak of the Second world war, and the uncertainty of what kind of attack our country would receive, Stamford like other cities and towns began taking air raid precautions. I have been unable to find any set guidelines, but I imagine that Miss Taylor would have taken the necessary action. To protect the Guests and the staff during an air raid, the hotel's cellars would have been an ideal place to adapt as a bomb shelter and all the windows needed taping to reduce cuts from splintering glass. The other problem we all experienced was a complete black-out of all windows, something the ARP wardens were very keen to keep enforced.

As the town was surrounded by army camps and a number of airfields, in the evenings and at weekends, a familiar sight was Army and RAF officers, together with American, Polish and other members of the allied forces, all of them using the George as a venue to get away from the troubles of war for a few hours.

With the great number being called up for war service the hotel would have relied on many older people working in the hotel. Food rationing was another headache for caterers, and I imagine guests would have to surrender valuable food coupons when they stayed away from home. Fortunately the George Hotel came through the war unscathed, there were two or three bombs at Burghley that damaged trees and windows and on the outskirts of the town, but Stamford's ancient town centre was left untouched.

In July 1945 George Adams, who was the gardener at the George during the war, invited two Land Army girls, Margaret Jones and Joan Banfield for tea. When he had to take his dog out, the two girls stole a pair of his shoes, they were eventually caught after stealing other goods and sent to prison for two months.

During the 1940s a notorious murderer stayed at the George hotel when he visited the town. He was John George Haig, the infamous acid bath killer who was hung for his horrific crimes in 1949. John was born in the town in 1909 his parents living in Kings Road.

In the early 1950s, the George Hotel was acquired by a private company run by, The Earl of Gainsborough, who was chairman and Mr John P.C Danny, who was the managing director. It was advertised as: A famous old Coaching Inn on the Great North Road full of historical interest with a beautiful Monastery Garden, facilities, Central Heating hot and cold water in all bedrooms. Lock up Garages, moderate terms. RAC and AA appointments. The telephone was No. 2102

It was in the 1953 when the York Room Bar (as it is now) was restored to commemorate the Coronation. The plaster ceiling was removed and the original oak beams uncovered. The red upholstery adds a sense of warmth to the room, and there is a set of prints of 18th Century racehorses. On one wall there stands a model coach and horses of the same period. When the old ceiling was removed the remains of 6 churchwarden's clay pipes were uncovered. A Churchwarden, was the name given to a long stemmed tobacco pipe made of clay, and the manager Mr J. Hardman said that one was half full of tobacco.

The London Room

The York Room Bar

The London room being a Lounge richly panelled from floor to ceiling. Other alterations carried out at this time were, the old Tudor room into the cosy Television Lounge. The charming Dining Room combines harmoniously with the Central Heating, bed rooms with hot and cold water, some with private bathrooms. The cuisine is a special feature, and the kitchen garden provides much of the requirements for fruit and vegetables. The wines being stored in ideal conditions in the vaults.

The Season's Greetings

from the

GEORGE HOTEL STAMFORD

CHRISTMAS EVE
CHRISTMAS DAY
CHRISTMAS SUNDAY
BOXING DAY

Menu

LUNCHEONS
AND
DINNERS

APPETIZERS

Smoked Scotch Salmon	4/6
Shrimp or Lobster Cocktail	3/6
Half Grapefruit & Maraschino	1/6
Orange & Grapefruit Cocktail	1/6
Various Fruit Juices	1/-
Clear Veal Broth with Sherry	1/6
Cream of Asparagus	1/-
Cream of Mushroom	1/-

FISH

Grilled River Trout in Caper Butter 3/6
Fried Halibut Steak in Bernaise Style 3/6
Fried Fillet of Plaice, Tartare Sauce 3/-

CHRISTMASTIDE, 1954

MAIN DISHES

ROASTS

Surrey Chicken: Bread Sauce ... 5/6
Aylesbury Duckling: Apple Sauce 6/6
Norfolk Turkey: Chipolata Sausages 6/-
Leg of Pork: Sage & Onion Stuffing 5/-
Fillets of Veal in Viennese style... 6/6

COLD TABLE

Sirloin of English Beef: Horseradish Sauce 5/-
Hindquarter of Lamb: Mint Sauce 5/-
Cumberland Ham: Mustard Sauce 5/-
Scotch Salmon Mayonnaise ...... 6/6 And Salad
Half Cornish Lobster 6/6

VEGETABLES

Buttered French Beans: Green Peas
Braised Celery Hearts—all at 9d.

POTATOES

Croquette   French Fried
Roast   Creamed—all at 9d.
A choice from the Fruit Basket... 1/6

SWEETS

Christmas Pudding: Brandy Sauce 2/6
Hot Mincemeat Pies: Whipped Cream 1/6
Yule Log Gateau 1/6
Pear Melba 2/-
Neapolitan Ice Gateau 1/6
Stewed Fruits & Ice Cream 1/6
Apples : Gooseberries : Blackcurrants
Vanilla : Strawberry : Chocolate
Ice Cream

SAVOURIES

Stuffed Olives Rolled in Bacon ... 3/-
Grilled Mushrooms on Toast ... 3/-
Welsh Rarebit 2/-
The Cheese Board: Biscuits & Celery 1/6

(Camembert : Gruyere
Cheddar : Stilton)

COFFEE 1/-

— Printed by The Panther Press, Cheyne Lane, Stamford. —

A Menu from Christmas 1954

For two years a Devonshire farmer Kenneth Potter became resident director of the George Hotel and with his wife Sarah they managed the hotel from 1955 to 1957, when they moved to the Haycock Hotel at Wansford.

It was in 1957 that, for the first time in the history of the Hotel the public were being offered shares in the company of which the Earl of Gainsborough was the company chairman, and Mr John P. C Danny, a Barrister was managing director. Mr Danny said that people from all over the world, going from London to Scotland, called at the George and its reputation was spoken of wherever such travellers met. The hotel stands in nearly three acres of land, and has a dining room which will seat eighty people, and there are fifty one bedrooms .

As the hotel is situated on the Great North road ninety miles from London it is an ideal stopping place for travellers after about 2½ hours driving. Being open day and night, people are able to come in any time. At weekends, parents visiting their children at boarding schools in Stamford, Oakham and Uppingham became guests at the George. It was quite common that often there would be 100 people waiting for tables in the dining room on Sundays. The hotel was eventually owned by Grovewood Securities, of London.

During the summer of 1961 couples were invited to dine and dance at the George every weekend, from 8.30pm until midnight. A time to celebrate that special occasion 15/-, that's 75 pence, plus 10% inclusive for a very special meal. Dress was optional, but please book in advance. Telephone 2102.

To celebrate Stamford's Quincentenary in 1961. The Stamford Amateur Stage and Madrigal Group staged, a Midsummer's Night Revels in the Monastery Garden at the George on Saturday evening 24th June at 8.15 pm. They were performing Elizabethan Madrigals and scenes from Shakespeare.

Admission was by Programme 4/- and 2/6 available at the gate or from F.J McIntosh in Ironmonger Street.

A former Premier of France, who was holidaying with some friends in England during August 1961, stopped at Stamford as they were on their way to Scotland. Monsieur Antoine Pinay and Madame Pinay, with their two friends Monsieur and Madame Goute made the George Hotel their overnight stop. They spent the evening walking around and admiring the ancient buildings, he thought our beautiful city was so peaceful and quiet, compared with Paris.

The summer of 1961 was also the beginning of The Burghley Horse Trials, three day event and of course the George was fully booked up with riders and officials together with people who were spectators at this new and what has turned out to be a successful yearly event.

In 1962 the horse trials was not a happy occasion for Virginia Freeman-Jackson, as during her stay at the George she unfortunately had all her jewellery stolen from her room, and she also suffered a heavy fall from her horse, Irish Lace at the Waterloo Rails.

During the month of June in 1968 the first Stamford Arts Festival held their open-air production of Shakespeare's, A Midsummer Night's Dream in the Monastery Garden at the George Hotel. It was produced by Jean Harley and included over 60 amateur actors from Stamford, Peterborough, Oakham and Oundle. Many of the costumes were loaned by the Nottingham Playhouse, and in the historic garden of the George it was one of the most colourful spectacles ever presented in the town. There was covered seating for over 400 people and the event, which took place on June 25th to the 29th was very well attended.

A MIDSUMMER NIGHT'S DREAM

June 25th - 29th inclusive   8 p.m.

Monastry Garden, George Hotel

Covered accommodation for 400 people.
Tickets 6/-   Children and OAP 3/-
from: A.T. Brodie, St. Mary's Street: G.M Little, St. Peters Hill:
H.W Needham, Broad Street.
In aid of Mentally Handicapped Children.

Another year they re-enacted The Taming of The Shrew; we found a poster in the Art Centre Wine Bar but the year and prices had been folded under, or cut off.

The plays continued until 1971 when, The Stamford Shakespeare Company was formed and as the audiences grew larger they had to move from the George Hotel to their present location at Tolethorpe Hall.

In the late 1960s I have been told a Mr and Mrs Richardson were the managers of the George but I don't have any other information about them.

It was in 1971 when two brothers, Martin and Lawrence Hoskins of the Poste Hotel group, acquired the George Hotel from the Grovewood Securities of London.

In a guide of the late 1970s:
A fine Historic Coaching Inn, accommodating 90 persons in 50 rooms, one of which has a four

poster bed, and 26 of which have private bathrooms. All rooms have colour television, radio and telephone. The newest addition is a garden lounge, a handsome restaurant offering an a la carte menu, the main theme being carving wagons that offer roast sirloin of beef and other large joints every day.

Luncheon. 12.30 to 2.30pm. Dinner 7.00 to 10.30pm.

Other facilities include a cold buffet in our lounge every day, also bar snacks.

Accommodation for weddings, conferences, parties, business and social functions of all kinds.

The photograph of the York to London Royal Mail Coach

In the 1970s, an American based travel company decided to run an old mail coach from York to London, on a regular basis. The idea being for people to enjoy the experience of real coach travel in the 1800s.

On the maiden run the passengers complained so much of the uncomfortable ride they were experiencing, that the idea was immediately dropped.

A young lady has given me her memories of the George when she worked there from 1972 to 1975. In 1972 Sue was at school, but worked at weekends and during the school holidays, she then worked at the hotel for a full year.

The Chambermaid shifts started early and were 6.45am to 2pm: "A few times, on my way across the meadows to work, a Policeman would stop to ask me where I was off to that early in the morning. (Did he think that I was running away from home, as it would look as though I was heading towards the Station but would any one bother, these days?)" "I would explain to him that I had to be there early because there were x! amount of breakfasts to take up to the guests."

She says; "My duties included, Chambermaid, working in the Linen room, and Cleaner. We turned down the beds in the afternoon and served afternoon teas in the Still Room." "It was a really good place to work, when I was young. We made the work fun and involved the hotel and also the staff into our social lives."

One of the Linen room duties was counting the used linen napkins before bagging them up in sacks to send to the Bourne Laundry: "I can remember that last-nights food smell even today. The only perk about that particular job was, that occasionally, screwed up amongst the napkins, would be a £1 note!" (missed by the dining room staff when they were busy clearing the tables). "It was big money in those days, equivalent to the price of a sweet, from the menu."

"Ivo Vanocci was the manager of the George, with his wife Julia when I started to work there. He was good fun to work with and very fair to all his employees. He remembered everyone at Easter, giving each of us an Easter egg, then a bottle of wine, as a Christmas gift. Ivo employed a lot of Italian students from his home area in Tuscany. They would work at a variety of jobs in the hotel and then attend English lessons at Stamford College."

"Some of them lived-in at the hotel, or he found them flats and cottages around the town and some lived at the Stamford Hotel in St. Mary's Street; Mary Clayton was the housekeeper in charge of the Stamford Hotel, but it was a bit spooky there, so you didn't hang around much on your own."

Ivo Vannocci was born in the small village of Lilliano in Italy. In the late 1960s, after working in London at the Savoy hotel and Great Yarmouth, he then became resident director at the George Hotel. Ivo and his wife Julia, who comes from Suffolk, have brought a blend of artistic technical and quiet efficient welcome to the establishment. "We treat our guests as family."
He went on to say that although some may have high-flown titles, other may be popular stars of TV or films, whilst others just ordinary folk having a weekend holiday. "They all deserve and are entitled to the best we can give, and everybody who works for us believes this and helps it to happen." This is perhaps the secret of his success.

"When Ivo became a director of the Poste Hotels group, in the mid 1970s, Richard Gorrie became the manager with his wife Janet." They went on to run the Garden House Hotel some years later.

"Patrick Kelly was a very efficient Head Porter who worked at the hotel from the late 1960s until the early 1970s. Ivo respected and thought very well of Pat, as did all the staff and guests to the hotel. The George continued to help him into his retirement."

"William Morgado took over the position of Head Porter from Pat, he also ran the "George Tap" with the help of his wife Rosa." The "Tap" was closed in 1981 when it became part of the new Business and Conference centre. William's elder son was employed at the hotel as a chef. William left the George Tap to run the "Bull and Swan" Inn St. Martins for several years. He then ran the "Royal Oak" at Duddington, until he retired to his home in Portugal a couple of years ago.

"When I started working at the George - Chris Pitman was a chef there and he is still there some thirty years later!"

"There was a man called "Henry" and he managed the "Cocktail Bar," A very dry character and the bar was always known as "Henry's Bar." He was good at his job, but did not like the staff to fraternise with visitors and residents in his domain."
"All cooked meals were provided for the staff, whilst they were on duty." Mrs Pinder was the Staff Cook.

"Two more ladies, "Aunty" and "Sissie" who ruled the Still Room. Both short, but fully in charge, (and kind hearted underneath). Just try to walk from the kitchen, across their recently mopped floor, to Reception, *If You Dare!*"

"The staff was an International mixture of temporary, permanent, and local people, with an emphasis on the young, although some have remained with the hotel for many years."

"They covered all the jobs in the Hotel "front and back." Reception, porters, bar staff, dining room staff, cleaners, chambermaids, linen room, kitchens, pot wash, gardeners etc."

The York bar is supposed to have tunnels going to St. Martins Church and also to Burghley House. There was also supposed to be a secret door into one of the tunnels in the Lincoln Room.

"When the Burghley Horse Trials were on in the early 1970s, I did see Princess Anne when she stayed at the George during the event. I had to spring clean, prepare and clean her bedroom whilst she was in residence."
"And yes, I did have to ask Richard Meade, who was a famous competitor in those days, if he would move, please! You see, he was sitting across the stairs chatting with Captain Mark Phillips, and I was trying to get downstairs with the industrial hoover cleaner."

She ends by saying "Yes, they were good old days especially the "Tap" on Payday!"

In 1979 it was a Vintage year for 18 year old Kate Pulvetaft, manageress of the bar snacks and buffet at the Hotel. A former pupil of Peterborough Girls County School, she had gained top marks in a course for the Poste Hotels employees on wines. She gained 92 per cent in the exam of the Guild of Wine School for Sommeliers, gaining a diploma with distinction. She said "We do sell a lot of wine at the George Hotel, it's one of those things which goes towards making a meal enjoyable." And Michael Waycot the general manager added: "We are very pleased that the top marks went to an employee from the George."

When the Burghley Horse Trials was a team competition, the British team always stayed at the George. In the 1974 Horse Trials on the evening before the cross country event, Chris Collins and others were summoned to colonel Bill Lithglow's bedroom at the George, where they found him painfully propped up in a chair, suffering from five ribs that were broken in Tuesday evening's donkey race. He was however able to give them a detailed and thorough briefing for the next day.

The 1977 horse trials, was a year to remember for Lucinda Prior-Palmer. She was staying at the George and on the Friday she had an early start, so Colonel Bill Lithglow picked her up at 7.15am and drove her from the hotel to the cross-country course. Her horse George put on a wonderful performance before the crowds of people, and managed to win the Individual Gold Medal, and for Britain the European Team Title.

The guests at the hotel were entertained by a concert of 18th Century and modern music in the historic Garden Room in the summer of 1979. The concert was given by nine pupils of the Stamford High School, all members of the school orchestra, who played Mozart and Beethoven and sang folk songs and Latin American songs, supervised by their director of music Mr Ian H. Alcoran. The concert, held on three evenings during the week, was arranged to entertain guests visiting the East of England show at Alwalton, Peterborough.

The George has been awarded many accolades during its long existence:
In 1980, The Good Food Hotel Guide: "A well run Hotel with superb dining room and various interesting bars and courtyard. The food was superb, speciality sirloin of beef, a beautiful oak beamed lounge with a roaring log fire in the winter. A personal service to a degree that is exceptional these days. Makes a memorable place to stay in a town worthy of more notice, it is located in the town centre and has parking for 150 cars."
Terms: B&B. £15.50 to £18. Special weekend breaks. Early October until April.

Afternoon Tea in the Garden Room on Thursday 6th March 1980, was accompanied by spring's new fashions, when Sugar and Spice of Stamford Walk, the ladies dress shop, held their fashion show at the George. The proprietor Mrs Diana Steele showed town wear, casual wear evening wear and special occasions clothes, with labels including Poppy, Sans Doute and Parigi. There was a bridal section with bridal gowns from Bridal Scene of Ironmonger Street, Stamford.

On Friday 28th March 1980. The George Hotel's general manager Michael Waycot organised an Antique weekend. The well known TV presenter John Bly gave a talk on, The Englishman's Home Through the Ages and Christopher Pringle, The life and Times of Robert Adam. The 45 guests who were on the package weekend, also took part in a guided walk around Stamford.

Some of the Hotel staff were in a Festive mood in 1980 for the first Stamford Carnival and Parade, which starts Stamford Festival Week in July. Their float was the re-creation of the interior of the foyer of the Hotel with their fattest ever customer, Daniel Lambert, impersonated by Chris Swan, a mere 20 stone and with a lot of padding. Two serving wenches were on hand, and a chef busily carved turkey, most of which Chris consumed, Chris was a regular at the Inn.
They managed however to carry off the runners-up prize.

The hotel's General manager Michael Waycot married Sally Ann Woodhead of Empingham at St Augustine's Roman Catholic church in Stamford, on the 1st August 1980 and after their honeymoon the couple set up home in St. Paul's Street, Stamford.

In the latest edition of Egon Ronay's, Just a bite guide for the summer of 1981, The George of Stamford was awarded the good tea symbol, a teapot. The award, introduced for the first time in 1981 was given to establishments that served a good quality cup of tea. "A good cup of tea has become a rare find, for two reasons: the public is not discerning enough and caterers do not seem to realise that the cost difference between good quality and insipid tea is negligible." Said Egon.

On the 6th March 1981 the hotel held another of its Antique Weekends. On Friday evening there was a talk on Stamford, given by Dr Eric Till, a local historian and a respected doctor in the town. Over the weekend John Bly's subject was Victorian furniture and Henry Sandon of the Royal Worcester Museum, also a regular TV presenter talked on Porcelain. Visitors brought along pieces to be identified. The residential weekends incorporated a Mediaeval style dinner, with the guests being serenaded by the Rutland Revellers. Another weekend was arranged for the end of the month.

The first weekend in April, Richard Gorrie had organised an Introduction to Archaeology at the hotel. A weekend of talks intended to provide the interested layman with a few insights into the world of modern archaeology. The tutors were Francis Pryor MA, FSA and Maisie Taylor MA. The cost for the weekend was £60, which also included accommodation and meals.

In 1981 Major conversion work on the Hotel Tap and the old stable buildings were started to turn the site into a prestige Business and Conference Centre, at an estimated cost of £80,000. The work on the building has left the old stone outside intact to blend in with the rest of the hotel, parts of it dating back to 1597.

Mr Lawrence Hoskins said "It is a complete business complex for the businessman, a suite of rooms specifically for that purpose." The ground floor of the building features three executive offices, two boardrooms, copy and telex facilities and secretarial services. A computer cable link allows businessmen to bring along a laptop and have access to their own main computers for immediate data and information. A complete range of audio-visual equipment, registration staff for meetings and direct dial telephones, complete the impressive list of services available.
The first floor of the complex has a 60 seater conference room with full projection and audio

visual facilities and also a foyer area, toilets and a small bar. The centre can also be used by local organisations and clubs.

The George hotel also went through an improvement scheme, new carpets, furniture and major re-upholstery work went on in the dining room and lounge, also 14 new en suite bathrooms. The housekeeper Mrs Idena Brandrick and Mrs Julia Vannocci, have been closely involved with the improvement operation, which has included a new central heating system. "We are determined that the George is going to be one of the best provincial hotels in England," said Lawrence Hoskins.

The Hotel were offering a Complete Wedding Service in April 1982, to save time, trouble and expense and a risk of booking with an unreliable firm, we are able to recommend suppliers of wedding cakes, cars, stationery, photographs and flowers.

We offer flowers for the reception in order to complete the atmosphere, designed by the hotel to complement the dress material chosen for the Bridesmaids. There is first class accommodation, for guests who wish to stay overnight. A changing room can be provided for the bride and groom at no extra cost, to enable them to change prior to their departure. A quotation for the reception is likely to be less expensive than you imagine, as there are no charges for the room in which the reception is held.

Selecting the Menu. The Wedding Breakfast can take many forms but it appears that the carved buffet creates an atmosphere that enables the bride, the groom and their parents to circulate freely among guests. The buffet consists of joints of beef, turkey, hams, decorated salmon etc., together with various hors d'oeuvres, salads and sweets.

Choosing the Wines and Drinks for your guests, a few suggestions: On arrival, (served after greeting your guests) sherry a choice of dry, medium or sweet. Sparkling wine can be served on arrival and continued through the reception and toasts. Alternatively our house red, white or rose may be served with the buffet, followed by champagne for the toasts. Naturally a good selection of soft drinks, squashes and colas are always available for the children and drivers.

Royal diners at the George Hotel on a Sunday in the early 1980s: Prince and Princess Michael of Kent lunched at the George with Lord and Lady Northampton, they joined 79 others diners in the hotel's main dining room.

The George Hotel went to great lengths to transport the Beaujolais Nouveau on its last leg of the journey in November 1982. Using a boat the wine was brought up the River Welland and then hoisted over the town bridge. Hotel staff were dressed in traditional French berets and striped trousers. Accompanied by an accordion player they wheeled the wine into the hotel on a cart adorned with French delicacies. Guests, who included the Town Mayor, Councilor Mrs Mary Gray and consort, and Town Clerk Mr Denis O'Leary, and his wife, then enjoyed a typical Burgundian breakfast in the hotel's garden lounge.

There was a change of Hotel manager in December 1982, when the staff gave a farewell party to Richard and Janet Gorrie. Richard Gorrie first joined the George in June 1971 as assistant manager then becoming the hotel manager in 1980. Mr. Ivo Vannocci the George's director said: "I have worked with many people but have found very few who are so hard working, generous and loyal as Richard". He gave them a personal gift of an antique, cut glass dressing table bottle. Gifts from the hotel staff included a leather desk set, two champagne glasses and a bouquet of flowers for Janet Gorrie. Mr and Mrs Gorrie took over St. Martin's Garden House Hotel in Stamford from January 1983.

Mr. Gorrie's replacement at the George was Mr Jolyon Gough, who for the past three years had been marketing manager at the four star Grand Hotel in Torquay. "I am very excited about this appointment, and will try to develop the wonderful foundations Richard has left, with particular emphasis on developing local trade for the hotel and promoting the new business centre."

A Menu from Vokes Dinner Party

February 1983

Vokes Ltd. Are a company who produce and market a range of filters and filtration systems to industry, they were fitted to Blackstones of Stamford diesel engines.

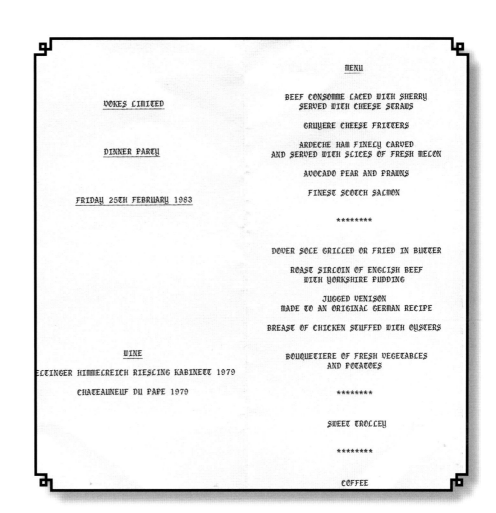

VOKES LIMITED

DINNER PARTY

FRIDAY 25TH FEBRUARY 1983

WINE

ELTINGER HIMMELREICH RIESLING KABINETT 1979

CHATEAUNEUF DU PAPE 1979

MENU

BEEF CONSOMME LACED WITH SHERRY
SERVED WITH CHEESE STRAWS

GRUYERE CHEESE FRITTERS

ARDECHE HAM FINELY CARVED
AND SERVED WITH SLICES OF FRESH MELON

AVOCADO PEAR AND PRAWNS

FINEST SCOTCH SALMON

****

DOVER SOLE GRILLED OR FRIED IN BUTTER

ROAST SIRLOIN OF ENGLISH BEEF
WITH YORKSHIRE PUDDING

JUGGED VENISON
MADE TO AN ORIGINAL GERMAN RECIPE

BREAST OF CHICKEN STUFFED WITH OYSTERS

BOUQUETIERE OF FRESH VEGETABLES
AND POTATOES

****

SWEET TROLLEY

****

COFFEE

Cellarman, Arthur Wallhead has rolled out his last barrel, at the age of 82. He decided to call it a day after looking after the Hotel's beer for 15 years. He would always come in at the dot of 6.30am every morning and worked through until noon. "However much we have tried to make him have days off, he always comes in every day, and he never liked to take holidays," said Jolyon Gough, the Hotel manager.

So in June 1984 they gave Arthur a Champagne retirement party, to wish him well, he received several gifts from his colleagues plus a silver tankard, and an open invitation to visit the hotel as a guest for lunch or a drink at any time from the George management.

The same evening there was more champagne celebrations at the Hotel as 20 year old wine waiter Charles Kentish received at magnum of champagne from Krug, for selling the most bottles of their champagne during Christmas.

In 1984, it was SUMMERTIME at the GEORGE. There was a Courtyard Barbecue including charcoal grilled steak, french fries, mixed salad from £5.95. This was held every evening, subject to weather.

Garden Lounge Buffet: A delicious selection of cold carved meats and salads, available every Lunchtime and Evening.

Spectacular ice creams and sorbets: choose from a selection of fabulous Italian ice creams and sorbets, including bananarama, venetian gondola, and sorbet seduction.

The York Bar: Now serving Stella Artois Lager.

On Friday the 17th August in 1984 they also held a Georgian Musical Evening, Featuring Robert Aldwinkle on Harpsichord, playing Arne Sonata No 4. Handel's Fantasia in C Sarabande. Then Michael Blankley read, The Poetry and Verse of John Clare (John was a local poet who was born at Helpston).

Nigel Dixon sang a selection of Georgian Glee Songs.

Tickets cost £2 each and there was a licensed Bar from 7.30 to 9.30pm.

In a top quality hotel like the George you expect the staff to conduct themselves always in an exemplary manner, which they always do. But on a Saturday evening in March 1987 things did get out of hand. The punch-up started in a passageway leading from the dining room, just before midnight, diner Richard Russell, from Easton-on-the-Hill was drinking coffee after a meal when he saw fists fly. He said, "I couldn't believe my eyes, it was just like watching a scene from the TV series Fawlty Towers. We were having a quiet coffee after our meal when all hell broke loose." The wine waiter and the manager were in the corridor having a full-scale brawl. The assistant manager tried to sort it out and they went for him as well.

Mr Russell said when the fight ended the assistant manager came over, adjusted his cuffs, apologised and said he hoped it hadn't spoiled the night.

Hotel director Ivo Vanocci today apologised for the trouble. He said the staff involved had been called in to explain themselves but will not be disciplined. And he said; "It was very unfortunate and we are sorry that the customers were upset. The staff were under pressure because it was a busy Saturday night and things got on top of them. Words were exchanged and things flared up."

In September 1987 there was another change of General manager when Philip Newman-Hall took over the post from Jolyon Gough, who had moved to Stratford–on-Avon.

Philip Newman-Hall age 31 is from the Spa Hotel at Tunbridge Wells, where he was general manager. His wife Anne Marie was also trained in Hotel management and they met in the trade at Banbury. She had been an assistant manager and has joined Philip to work on the reservations and accounts at the George.

He has noticed already the difference between the area around Tunbridge Wells and Stamford, "It takes a long time to be accepted in that part of the world, but everyone here have been welcoming and friendly," he said. "The George is very much part of the community in Stamford and always will be, we will certainly maintain its traditions."

The George has always been ready to encourage youngsters who are interested in making the catering trade their career. In January 1988 pupils from the various schools in the town and area, were given a tour of the hotel to celebrate the Hotel and Catering Training Board's open day, after which they were then asked to compile a project. It was the Queen Eleanor school pupils who scooped the awards.

Teenagers Lucy Goossens (16) and Lee Parkes (15) wrote the best reports out of 21 entries.

Lucy, who wants to be an interior designer, was given a cookery book as first prize after studying the décor of the hotel. Lee, in second place has ambitions to go into catering and he wrote about the history of the ancient coaching Inn.

When the hotel manager Philip Newman-Hall handed over a £15 afternoon tea voucher to the winners at a special presentation. He said "They both have a very novel way of looking at the hotel. I have learned a lot by reading their projects."

BIG-HEARTED. Staff at the George Hotel delivered a special Valentine's Day surprise to residents at the Whitefriar's pensioner's homes. The staff handed out 100 red roses, which were greatly appreciated. Duty manager, Bridgett Copp with staff members, Francoise Perron, Nicola Hothershall and Ian Evans handed over the flowers, and also some to the Burghley Almshouses residents, which is opposite the Hotel. The silk roses were made by the Stamford High School Young Enterprise company.

"GOLDEN MEMORIES"

In April 1988, The staff at the George Hotel really made it a night to remember for a couple who celebrated their Golden Wedding anniversary at the hotel, exactly 50 years to the day when they slept in the Bridal Suite. The couple William and Jane Oakey, who were from Northamptonshire were not overcharged for their night at the historic Inn.

The celebrating pensioners produced their old bill for £1.12.6d dated April 18 1938, and were charged the equivalent amount in modern money £1.62. A spokesman for the George said: "We thought it would be a nice touch to make the evening extra special for them."

In June 1988 all the staff were shocked to learn of the loss of one of their younger colleagues: Adam Chick an 18 year old, who was employed as a cellarman was involved in a serious accident on Peterborough's Parkway during a freak storm on Friday afternoon. His girl friend, Ethiopian born Yordanos Fisseha travelling with him was also badly injured. His car collided with a lamp post and he had to be cut free. Miss Fiessha also works at the George. The staff at Addenbrooks Hospital in Cambridge did all they could for Adam, but sadly he died a week later. His devoted pals rallied round and raised over £1300 to donate to Addenbrooks as a token of appreciation for all their dedication.

The Hotel were sponsors for the Stones (Blackstones) youth football team, and in September 1988 Philip Newman-Hall, general manager of the George handed over new football kit for all the team, to Pete Thomas, who was their manager.

The Hotel staff were celebrating in style during November 1988 after hearing they not only picked up two accolades from Egon Ronay, the country's premier Gastronaut, but also three new awards from the RAC.

From Egon Ronay, the author of numerous eating out guides, comes "The Symbol of Excellence" for an outstanding Cheeseboard plus an Outstanding rating for the hotels cellar, and the RAC whose awards were only introduced this year, had recommended the George for its hospitality and service, comfort and restaurant.

General manger Philip Newman-Hall said, "We are absolutely delighted with all of these awards, particularly as this is the second year running we have been commended by Egon Ronay."

The George does not offer a wide selection of cheeses, for as executive chef, Chris Pitman explained. "Rather than have a lot of stock, which may go off before they are used, we prefer to offer just a few excellent cheeses." He uses four or five whole Stilton, three or four whole Brie and two or three 60lb Cheddars per week.

On the wine side, they stock 200 different varieties, including ones from America, Australia and New Zealand. They range in price from £6.45 to £165 a bottle and as Philip Newman–Hall explained. "We try to offer a good range of wine to suit all tastes and pockets."

"A lot of places put a huge mark up on their wines, but we try to keep our to a minimum to offer people the opportunity of sampling good wines at affordable prices. We have over 30 different ones on offer at under £10 a bottle." The hotel's cellar is home to everything from 1987 vintage wine to a bottle of port dating back to 1904. The George appears in The Good Food Guide, The Good Hotel Guide, The Which Wine guide and numerous others.

The starting point for the Fitzwilliam Hunt in March 1989, was the George, as building work was being carried out at their normal venue. More than 100 horses and hounds ran around in the hotel's courtyard as the riders sipped Bucks Fizz and ate a hearty breakfast. "This is the first time the George has been used as a staring point," said Philip Newman-Hall. "Everyone had a great time and we hope it will become an annual event".

In a recently run course by the South Kesteven County Council on the many aspects of hygiene, covering general food hygiene including storage, handling and preparation. One of the successful students was Sue Butcher from the George Hotel, who takes all aspects of hygiene seriously. She received her certificate in June 1989.

During July the George organised a competition for the pupils of Queen Eleanor School. All who took part donned chef's hats, the object being to create a swan from a tomato, and a fan by folding a napkin. The best entry by a boy and a girl, were rewarded with a £10 note. An umbrella was given to the most enthusiastic contestant. The winners were Lee Szymanski, Paul Spooner and Fay Rance. They all received their prizes from the judges, Philip Newman-Hall general manager, Matthew Durrant restaurant manager and Tony Tinkler chef at the George Hotel.

In August 1989 the Stamford Arts Centre and the George joined forces to present an exhibition of work by one of the country's top artists. The sculptures and wood carvings by David Gross of Fareham in Hampshire. The work was on display in the garden of the George and also at the Arts Centre.

Princess Anne's estranged husband Captain Mark Phillips was nicknamed "Captain Who?" as he kept a low profile during an equestrian event. When he checked into the George for the Burghley Horse Trials in 1989 he went unrecognised. A staff member at the hotel said: "A bell boy was asked to show Captain Mark Phillips to his room." The boy said, "which one is he?"
He stayed for a number of nights in a £64 a night room. Princess Anne frequently stayed at the George during her eventing career.

The local peoples friendly atmosphere offered to the Judges, officials, sponsors and well established guests has resulted in the George becoming a "Headquarters" for the horse trials. Philip Newman-Hall the hotel manager says: "You couldn't get a room here for the next 10 years, as most of the 47 rooms are permanently reserved for the event. Some of our guests have stayed here since the Burghley Horse Trials began."

Some of the pupils from Stamford's Queen Eleanor school were given an insight into the work of a chambermaid at the George during November 1989. Supervised by the head housekeeper Barbara Spottiswood they were put to bedmaking, maintenance and laundry portering, assisted by chambermaids - Shirley Gray and Judith Walker. Mrs Spottiswood said "they seemed to enjoy their experience and it certainly opened their eyes." The days begin at 6am when preparations for breakfast in the 47 roomed hotel begins.

A Wedding Fair was held on Saturday 11th November 1989, from 11.30am to 4.30pm. Stamford brides to be had a chance to organise everything for their big day under one roof. Dresses by Helen Kirkwood, China and Glass by Lambs, Photography by Paul Ranft, Cakes by Joan Milligan, Flowers by Bloomers, Printing by Glen Boughton, Entertainment by Steve Allen. In the courtyard a Rolls Royce limousine by Gold Lady Cars. Two of the models wearing Bridal gowns were, Jacqui Edwards and Wendy Barker.

At home preparations for the Christmas dinner takes some organising for the lady of the house, deciding on the size of the bird, how many of the family there will be on the big day. They usually start in early December, but just think of all the planning it takes to cook for the large numbers of people the hotel trade have to cater for.
Executive chef at the George, Chris Pitman said, "We start planning the menu for that year in January, that way Christmas is still fresh in our minds and we can change the menu accordingly." Chris has worked as a chef at the hotel for the past 18 years and cooked Christmas dinners for most of the years, "I enjoy working at Christmas. In fact it is probably one of the easiest days of the year because we have a set menu, but the days leading up to Christmas are the hardest because we have so many functions." He has 22 chefs working with him to make sure everything is right for the big day.

1989 to 1990 ended in a big spend at the George, all 200 places for Christmas lunch had been fully booked since July reported the manager Philip Newman-Hall, and 40 of the 47 rooms for the holiday and the New Years Eve dinner dance was fully booked.

There had been a lot of work getting all the decorations ready for the festive season, Julia Vannocci and her friend Dene have to start working on them in November, they have been responsible for all the wonderful decorations for a number of years, and all of them are original ideas.

One couple spent the night in a luxurious Four Poster Bed at the George in January 1990, to celebrate their tenth wedding anniversary. Bob and Lindsey Craig spent money given to them at Christmas by their parents on Hereward's Radio appeal, bidding £330 for a room at Stamford's top hotel, the George. The bubbly pair ate a champagne dinner before retiring to their regal bed. "We have been on a waterfall bed before, when we honeymooned at the Niagara falls, but never on a bed like this:" said Lindsey. The couple run kennels near Peterborough.

In April 1990 Philip Newman-Hall the general manager announced that he was leaving to take up a position with Richard Branson. Chris Pitman who had held the position as executive chef for 16 years was appointed general manager, and Carol Bettison was appointed to house manager.

This was the GEORGE HOTEL'S Team Summer 1990:

Operational Director, Ivo Vannocci. Executive Chef and Hotel Manager, Chris Pitman.
House and Service Manager, Carol Bettison. Senior Chef, Matthew Carroll.
Reservations Manager, Ulf Ortmann. Restaurant Manager, Edward Watson-Williams.
Hotel Secretary, Lynn Jones. Receptionist, Nicola Clayton, also 6 staff.
Housekeeper, Diane Dickson. Assistant Housekeeper, Nicholas Bray, also 19 staff.
Head Garden Lounge Chef, John Vant. Pastry Chef, Caroline Sayers also 14 Chefs.
Sous Chefs, Raymond Aubrey, Richard Stokes, Tony Tinkler, and 20 Cleaning staff.
Assistant Restaurant Managers, Steven Smith, Nicola Stokes also 15 staff.
Garden Lounge Manager, Angela Durrant. Assistant Garden Lounge Managers, Richard Dorman, Jackie Tinkler also 32 staff. Bars, 7 staff. Business Centre Manager, Helen Dale also 4 staff.
Hotel Seamstress, Maria Harrison. Porters, 6 staff. Head Gardener, Ernie Williams also 3 staff.
Car Park Security, Jim Dolby.

And here are just a few statistics. In the restaurant they serve 8 ½ miles of bread, 16,500 pounds of beef, 6,250 gallons of wine and they look after 34,000 people in a year.

Paul Burke a cellarman age 20 years was very enthusiastic talking about the wines in his keeping. As he handled a bottle of Chateau Mouton Rothschild priced at £85 a bottle he said "the cellar's beautiful and it's the oldest part of the hotel. The secret of running a good cellar is organisation, knowing where everything is, and keeping the place the same temperature throughout the year."

In June 1990 Simon Singlehurst, organised Ghost walks in Stamford. They were held every Friday evening at 8pm, the starting point was the George Hotel and the walk which lasted about an hour finished at the George. It attracted about 35 people and was going to continue until the weekend of the Burghley Horse Trials.

Julia's Dish of the Day. A Barnack teenager who won a competition organised by Stamford College and the George Hotel, gave her family a treat in August 1990.

As her prize, Julia Crowson aged 15, and a pupil of Kirkstone House School Baston, prepared and cooked her meal, as dish of the day at the George, and her family were invited to try it.

She also won a £50 voucher and a cookery book. The theme of the competition was to create a recipe using local products. Julia baked trout stuffed with almonds, peppers and chives.

Chris Pitman, the hotel's general manager who is always keen to give encouragement to the young sportsmen of the town, presented new kit to the Stones (Blackstones) youth football team in November 1990.

Lady Victoria Leatham, of Burghley House, was guest of honour at an opening ceremony for a new Boardroom at the George Hotel in February 1991. The Leatham Boardroom named after Lady Victoria, had been re-furbished to provide extra facilities for business executives due to the high demand at the hotel. It is equipped with the latest technology but still retains the traditional atmosphere of the George. Several members of the business community including local bank managers were invited to attend a champagne reception and the unveiling of the plaque.

Fiona Carr, of Personal Marketing and Training at the George said: "It was a very successful opening and Lady Victoria was pleased to have the room named after her." The event was hosted by Ivo Vannocci, Operations Director for The Poste Hotels Ltd and Chris Pitman, Executive Chef and Manager of the George Hotel.

Valentine's Day was full of surprises in 1991 for Miss Mercury. Miss Linda Johnson of Edenham, not only celebrated her 21st Birthday, but her boyfriend Gareth Evison proposed.

And on the Thursday night the couple were treated to a romantic meal at the George Hotel, where they even made Linda a birthday cake. Linda said "It was brilliant we had champagne and they sang Happy Birthday to me."

Four schoolgirls from the Stamford High School, who in the early part of 1991 took part in Nationwide Inter-schools competition organised by the Confederation of British Industry.

They studied all aspects of the George Hotel as their project interviewing staff and management. In May their efforts were well rewarded when it was announced, that they were runners-up in the competition. The four, Jenny Salmond, Alison Lilley, Laura Brown and Zoe Brown, had won £700 for their school and a rail trip to Glasgow. British Rail had sponsored the competition and in a ceremony at the George each of them were presented with their Confederation of British Industry Awards.

In September at the Burghley Horse Trials, Captain Mark Phillips was seen with a new Mystery woman. They were also seen, sitting side by side, enjoying a meal with four other people at Captain's Phillips table in the George Hotel.

November 1991. A special Cuisine Month in the Garden Lounge.

From Friday the 1st to Friday the 15th Thai Fortnight. An authentic Thai four course meal will be served at both Lunch and Dinner at £15.00 per person with a special guest appearance of Mr Ben, the most renowned Thai chef from Bangkok.

From Saturday the 16th to Saturday 30th Italian Food Festival. We have the return of our popular Italian evenings, offering a four course menu at £15.00 per person and on most evenings our Italian Duo will be performing live music.

"Win a night in Haunted Room 20." The George has a friendly ghost. Stamford Mercury Halloween supplement October 1992. Stamford's best known hotel is renowned for its luxury, good food and service, so it's just the place for a discerning ghost.

That's exactly what they've got between the ancient walls of the George, and the spook has a particular liking for room 20. Now in an exclusive Mercury competition, we are offering you a the chance to spend a free night there if you can prove you have got the nerve.

Many of the staff at the hotel can relate tales of the lady from number 20, but they are agreed she's not an evil spirit, in fact she is quite friendly and just right for your first brush with the hereafter. "The room is a lot colder than all the others, even though it has only one outside wall and we turn the heating right up," says control and purchasing manager Caroline Emerson. She adds: "A lot of the maids who change the room say they can feel something. It's a friendly feeling, but still a bit frightening."

The hotel's exclusive guest does not confine her wanderings to room 20. She has been known to take a stroll out of the room, down the stairs and into the lounge, where she disappears into the alcove by the fireplace.

Can you brave the spirit world and stay put where others have bottled out? If you would like the idea of spending the night with a ghost, tell us in no more than 100 words, why. (This was what was asked in the competition).

In November 1992. When the Daniels Football Team held their Social and Buffet evening, for directors, players, friends and sponsors, Chris Pitman and his wife Mary, presented new shell suits for the team to use on match days on behalf of The George Hotel.

A Christmas cake with a difference greeted visitors at Christmas in 1992. Head pastry chef Carolyn Sayers, rustled up her chocolate, sugar and marzipan treat and then put it in the hotel's foyer. "We wanted to brighten up the area in a slightly different way. Decorating cakes is part of my job, so that's what we decided on." Said Carolyn, who has worked at the George for three years. The decoration shows a scene of a log cabin, snow, snowmen and good old Santa going down the chimney.

Cupid Strikes Again, Valentine's Day 1993. Cupid's arrow hit the mark when Mark Evans proposed to his girl friend Dawn Edwards. Mark placed a Valentine greeting in the Mercury saying; "I asked you last year, you have had a year to think, make my day and say yes." Over a romantic dinner for two at the George on Sunday Mark reminded Dawn of the message and she did indeed make his day and say yes. "I booked a meal for the two of us on Valentine day and I had the staff bring a ring and a bottle of champagne to the table," said Mark, who lives at Edith Weston. "It was a total surprise for Dawn and we had a lovely time at the George."

In February 1993 firemen praised the quick thinking of the staff at the hotel. A fire in a rubbish bin was first discovered by Shirley Dean of the book-shop in the George Mews. She notified the hotel staff, who immediately sprang into action. Service manager Paolo Bianchi and Housekeeper Nick Bray dragged the bin away from the danger area and extinguished it before the fire brigade arrived. Hotel Director Ivo Vannocci said "We are very pleased that the fire precautions we practice have worked."
A spokesman for the Fire Brigade said "The staff were able to avoid what could have been a dangerous fire, because of quick thinking."

In December 1993 the dining room at the George was packed with diners waiting to see fashions and ball gowns from The Frock Exchange, a company from Fenstanton and Cottesmore. The style of the Mannequin parade was based on the 1950s, when models paraded amongst the tables so the diners could see the gowns at close quarters. The compere John Mason had to announce there would be a delay as one of the models was stranded in a traffic jam on the A1 somewhere between Huntingdon and Stamford.
Helena Walker a veterinary surgeon, who had gone to the hotel for a quiet dinner found herself star of the show, as she was picked from half a dozen lady diners who offered their services as a stand in. Shirley Mason of the Frock Exchange, who organised the show in conjunction with Mary Pitman said "We wanted someone who was the nearest size to our stranded model so we picked Helena."
Professional male model James paid tribute to his stand-in partner. He said "She was so natural that you would never have known this was her first modelling assignment."

The AA Rosette scheme, which was first introduced in January 1991, was awarded to the George Hotel in December 1993 for its very high standard of cuisine.
Out of 4,600 establishments that were inspected, only 1,233 had achieved the standard for a rosette award. A spokesman for the George said "We are very pleased to receive the award. Not many establishments achieve the rosette and this shows the high standard that the George offers."

In February 1994 two members of the food serving staff, Kyra Baker and Graham Candish were the first at the George Hotel to be awarded National Vocational Qualifications (NVQs).

To receive the prestigious Level 2 food service certificate both had to show a high level of competence when carrying out their work. Group training coordinator Mrs Sue Rudkin said "They had to work very hard because all the effort has to come from within." She hopes that more staff will follow Kyra and Graham's lead.

The magazine Sew Today used the George for their photography session in spring 1994. They found the Four Poster Bedroom was the ideal place to shoot their Heirloom Nightie and Lovely Lingerie range. They had intended to use the Courtyard for the remaining two outfits, as it was raining at the time they used the Reception area and the Garden Lounge with its exotic plants.

David Landry who lives in St Ives near Huntingdon, was invited to join the hotel's management team, as their Financial Director in 1995.

Another year of awards for the staff at the George hotel to celebrate in October 1995.

They were voted Lincolnshire Hotel of the year in the Which Hotel Guide, favourable mentions in the Good Food Guide and Good Hotel Guide for 1995. Director Ivo Vannocci was a national winner in the Italian Wine list of the year 1994. All of which add up to a very good year for the George.

The hotel won the category C award, for wine lists between 20 and 30 Italian wines. "We are in the business of selling wine, and in the business of pleasing our customers," said Ivo Vannocci. Wines were priced accordingly he said, he had no desire to buy wines just for them to sit gathering dust in the cellar. The present wine list ranges from £7.50 to £75.

The George was represented at Stamford's pancake race in 1996, which had been postponed for a week as it was snowing on Shrove Tuesday. The competitors lined up at the starting line with frying pans at the ready. As they raced along the High street, shoppers cheered them on. Martin Cummings, who represented the George hotel, was first across the finishing line. When he received the prize of £10, he kindly gave it back to the Red Cross Society, who had organised the race.

During March 1996. The Hotel stepped back in time, when it took delivery of a very special beer. Barrels of Shire Horse Show World, Champions Choice, were taken to the Inn on a traditional Dray, drawn by two gentle giants from Brookfield's Shire Horses. The ale was specially brewed to commemorate the National Shire Horse Show and Congress, being held at the East of England Showground, Peterborough on the weekend of March 16th to the 17th.

It was also in March when on a Saturday night at the hotel, some youths who were being rowdy were asked to leave. There was a fracas and five members of staff and a guest were hurt, no one seriously. The police were called to assist in the affray, and in arresting five men, two of the policemen were injured, one so badly that he had to be sent home from duty.

With the hotel then returning to normal, the guests were then able to enjoy their evening.

During the summer of 1996, Stamford's town centre was taken over by the television crews in the making of TV series Middlemarch. Robert Hardy the well known actor who played the part of Arthur Brook, made the George Hotel his home during the shooting of the film.

The George holds its first, Civil Marriage January 1997

Jonathon Potter aged 25 and his bride Genevieve Wilks-Chase were the first couple to "Tie the Knot" at the Hotel. The marriage ceremony took place in the same room that Jonathon's grandfather had used as an office when he ran the hotel.

Jan Potter, (Jonathon's mother) who provided me with the information, said "The ceremony took place in a lovely room, everything went very well with their close family to witness it." Jonathon's grandfather, Kenneth B. Potter and his wife Sarah ran the hotel from 1955 to 1957 they then moved to the Haycock Hotel in Wansford, which Sarah ran after her husband had died. After the wedding ceremony Jonathon and Genevive held a wedding reception for 130 people at the Haycock in Wansford.

Emma Allen, a girl who has always loved working with food, left the Stamford High School wanting a career in Hotel and Catering management. Preferring the practical route to the profession she joined the Stamford Colleges Choices. She has now been at the George for one year and is learning all the aspects of the world of top quality food preparation. Emma has gained her NVQ, (National Vocational Qualification) level two in food preparation at college, and is now studying for the advanced level three.

TV Chef Ross Burden's favourite restaurant:

In Good Housekeeping magazine for April 1997 the popular TV chef Ross Burden who appeared in TV cookery shows, Ready, Steady, Cook, The Big Breakfast and also hosted his own shows, was asked: "Which essential ingredients would you take to a desert Island?" He said, "The island would be surrounded by sea, containing fish and shellfish, so I'd take lemon to flavour the fish, also garlic, a bottle of decent olive oil, cheese, pepper, coffee beans, and a case of fine Claret."

"Who would you like to take to dinner on the Island?" "I'd settle for Joanna Lumley, she's bright and beautiful."

"You're saved! Which restaurant would you head for and what would be your first meal?"

"Do I want to come back from paradise? If I were forced to come back to civilisation I would head straight for the George Hotel in Stamford, Lincolnshire, a beautiful coaching Inn."

The Rotary Club of Stamford have been meeting regularly at the George Hotel since 1947 and to celebrate the 50 years the hotel made a donation of £1,000 of sponsorship for the club's Golf Tournament in April 1997. Martin Ball, the Rotary Club fund raising committee member said "We have been supported over the years by the George Hotel in a number of ways, but this donation is very generous and we are grateful for it."

As you walk up the steps from the car park into the Monastery garden, on your left in the corner is a wooden seat.

"In loving memory of George Ernest Williams. Head Gardener 1976 to 1999."

This is the hotels tribute to a very gifted and wonderful man. Instead of retiring at the age of 65 George Ernest Williams worked as a gardener at the hotel for 25 years, before he died on March 15th 1999 at the age of 90 years.

Julia Vannocci of the George hotel said "The place seems really strange without him. It's going to take a long time for us to adjust. You just can't replace someone like George." So highly was he thought of that in 1980 the hotel paid for a mural to be created in honour of his work. Julia added "At the time, George didn't like it one bit, he said it made him look old. Guests at the hotel often comment on the mural and it will become a fitting way for us to remember him."

Rather than sit back and take it easy in his retirement, George joined the hotel at 65 years of age and worked there unfailingly, despite his faltering ill health. "He stayed right up until the end, we tried to tell him to spend more time at home as his condition worsened, but he insisted on coming in every day to tend the flowers and plants in the hotel. He was a very knowledgeable and dedicated man and in love with his job." George, who was a widely respected figure in the gardening industry, judged at Chelsea and Sandringham flower shows and worked at Burghley House and Harewood House near Leeds during his distinguished career.

Three of the hotels staff have celebrated prestigious honours in their fields in 1999. Chef de Partie, Gareth Thorpe, won the Anglia heat of the National Commis Rotisseur Competition 1999. He went on to take second place in the national final in London on April 13th. Supervisor in the Garden Lounge department Denise Chick and Porter Simon Holiday, have passed the Higher National Certificate of the Wines and Spirit Education Trust. Sue Rudkin the training officer at the George, stressed the rarity of staff passing the advanced exam.

A tip of the week in The Express May 22nd 1999. The Complainer Page:
When you go into a restaurant you should expect to enjoy two vital elements in your meal.
(1) The food (2) The service. If one is good and the other is bad, do not suffer in silence.
All too often the British behave like twitching rabbits and cower at the prospect of confrontation. The complainer said. "Last Sunday, I visited the George of Stamford, Lincs. Not only was the food very good, the service was outstanding. What a Joy. As regular readers of this column well know, I would not have accepted anything less."

The usual tranquillity of the George's Monastery Garden was shattered in the summer of 1999 when two croquet teams met for a spirited game with mallets, hoops and balls. Chris Pitman and Pierre Marechal were part of the Hotel team that took on a group of experienced players from the Stamford and district Round Table. The crunch match is set to become an annual event. A shield was presented to the champions, the Round Table team.
Chris Pitman said "We all learned some new things about the rules and strategy. It's seen as a genteel game but its actually quite tactical and cruel. You can employ dirty tactics of knocking opponents balls away to deny them points. It's really good fun to play. The match went well, hopefully we can find more teams to play during the year."

The end of the century was a very busy time again, with the hotel being full over the holiday. It was celebrated by an exceptionally grand dinner and dance, beginning at 8pm. The disco and live band played throughout the evening and a Scottish piper greeted in the new century.

The London Room, with it's rich oak panelling makes it an ideal venue for that special banquet or executive meeting.

Realxing and taking tea in one of the comfortable lounges, with it's original beams and fireplace.

The York Bar, oak beams and panelling and a collection of hunting prints.

21st Century

After 100 years of the car we are finding, as some people predicted, that it would take over the public transport system. Fortunately for the hotel, if their car park is full there is a large municipal one only a short distance away.

Communications have progressed and we are now in the age of computers, e-mail and the web. I will not try to predict what this century will bring!

In June 2000 that a team of some of the staff at the George took place in a Dragon race at Rutland Water. In all 18 teams took part and helped to raise around £10,000 for the National Deaf Children's Society.

Stylish dining is on the doorstep now the George has received, The Dining Pub of the Year award from the Good Food Guide 2003. Staff at the old coaching Inn in St. Martins, were celebrating last week when they were told of the award. And the atmosphere is not the only thing that has firmly planted it in the guide as Lincolnshire Dining Pub of the Year. Food and drink are essential.

The Licensees of the George, Chris Pitman and Ivo Vanocci were thrilled with their achievement and said, "It is particularly rewarding for the hotel staff to be recognised for their hard work and dedication in achieving this accolade."

The George took a step back in time on Sunday the 7th December 2003.

The traffic stopped and along Station Road, there was the sound of a Post Horn and into the yard at the rear of the Inn came an 1830s mail coach. The coach was pulled by four magnificent white horses and was filled, inside and out, with passengers all dressed in clothes of the early 19th Century period. When the whip, guard and passengers had alighted, the young ladies from the Inn brought round some delicious mince pies, and a stirrup cup of warm punch ladled from their silver punch bowl. An added festive touch was the rows of Christmas trees that were all lit up in the courtyard.

Then after the spectators had taken photographs, they set off again with the post horn sounding into Station Road, then turning right and going under the Gallows sign, which in its time has had countless coaches travelling beneath it, up the High Street in St. Martins and across the park to Burghley House. This was all part of Stamford's Christmas Festivities, which had an Arts and Crafts Market on the same day, together with a visit from Father Christmas.

One of the en-suite rooms, tastefully furnished and complete with every convenience.

The ultimate room, a four poster bed with everything a guest would need.

The summer of 2004 has been a busy one for the George. In July to August the town was once again a film set, when St. Mary's Street and St. George's Square were taken over for the filming of Pride and Prejudice, some of the famous actors and actresses made the George their home whilst the filming was in progress. Their names have not been revealed, but Dame Judy Dench, Keira Knightly and Donald Sutherland were all in the cast.

Throughout August the Hotel hosted on an average of two weddings each week. David Landry, the finance director said, "The George was fully booked over the Burghley Horse Trials weekend as we are known so far a field and are part of Stamford's Heritage and History."

The general manager Chris Pitman said. "As usual we were fully booked and all the fine weather resulted in every day being a Saturday." They did a roaring trade and even ran out of champagne, more meals were served than usual and good weather meant that the courtyard was used to the full. In the Monastery garden a large marquee was put up for about 600 people to have drinks. After all this they felt a good rest was needed.

There were more accolades to celebrate later in the year. In October they were awarded the Hotel Bar of the Year title. Then in the Good Pub Guide for 2005, the George was chosen as Lincolnshire's Dining Pub of the year. The guide said that the elegant old and well known coaching inn produced very good food, with some excellent wines. The staff were friendly and attentive, and the bedrooms were very comfortable.

The staff were celebrating again in November when their excellent standard of service was recognised by the RAC. They were presented with the prestigious Blue Ribbon award, this is recognised throughout the industry as a mark of very high quality standards in food, service, hospitality and comfort.

Christmas time is always a very busy time at the George, local firms in trade and industry and associations remember the loyalty of their staff with an annual Dinner and Dance.

The Stamford Fat Stock Show which until the Foot and Mouth crisis caused the closure of the cattle market, was always held in the first week of December. The show was well supported by the local farmers and a local Butcher Peter Johnson, (now retired) remembers it in the 1930s. After the show was over there was a dinner at the George and this year, as you will see by the menu below, they enjoyed an excellent meal and entertainment.

FATSTOCK DINNER

MONDAY 6 DECEMBER 2004

MENU

Finest smoked Scottish salmon

Leek and potato soup

oOo

Roast sirloin of English beef with

Yorkshire pudding

Selection of vegetables and potatoes

oOo

Christmas pudding

The George's Sherry trifle

oOo

Stilton and brie served with biscuits,

grapes and celery

oOo

Coffee

Christmas and the old year went out in Venetian style this year 2004. As the guests arrived through the courtyard entrance they were greeted by a full size gondola and gondolier, the gondola carrying festive gifts. In the lounge 100 yards of silk were used to make silk panels and arches, with 200 decorated masks imported from Venice. There were also Canaletto style paintings and other touches to create the Venetian atmosphere.

New Years Eve's, Gala Dinner and Dance was another sell-out at £165 per person in the Restaurant and £148 per person in the Garden Lounge.

The evening began with a champagne reception at 7.30pm. As the guests arrived they were greeted by Sonny Monks and his jazz Band. There was a live band and disco playing throughout the evening, during a gourmet dinner. At midnight a Scottish piper was present to greet the New Year. The whole evening was a complete success.

Chris and Mary Pitman are an ideal couple to run the hotel, and they always try to give their best to the customer. Chris is Executive Chef and Manager, and he comes from Leicester but has worked at the George for over 30 years. Mary is a Stamfordian who deals more with the customers and staff with whom she is on Christian name terms. She was telling us that the new kitchen is now in use. It was handmade in France of solid stainless steel and is every chef's dream. The kitchen also has air conditioning making the chef's working conditions as comfortable as possible. They do care deeply about the hotel and would like it always to remain family owned.

The George of Stamford, experience. Are you a regular, or have you never walked into the foyer?

To walk into the George is going into a different world. The foyer gives you an immediate feeling of being relaxed, with the old panelling and very comfortable chairs, all placed at random and there is always someone to welcome and help you with any of your questions.
The staff, from the helpful young ladies in reception, right through to Chris and Mary Pitman are available to ensure your time spent in the hotel is a unique experience. Although you realise that you are in a very beautiful and old establishment nothing is old fashioned, but care is taken with all aspects of furnishing, which give you the feeling that the rooms have been, lovingly restored in the very best of taste.
When we took lunch in the garden restaurant, we found the staff very helpful and friendly, the salad we choose was excellent and the food was ample, with a pot of coffee to finish and have a chat. The restaurant was busy as usual but with plants screening the tables you were not overlooked and could listen to the delightful chatter of people enjoying their meal and each others company.

It is nice to meet in the courtyard to take coffee or tea, with a mouth-watering selection of cakes or sandwiches that the George have to offer. When the sun gets hot the colourful umbrellas allow you to enjoy your food and drink in some shade.

From the courtyard you pass under the archway, and where there was once coach houses, and stables, then later garages. These buildings too have all been re-developed with care and attention, so they are still in keeping with the rest of the hotel.

On the left hand side are a number of shop units:

Firwood Design's: They are noted for their hand painted silks, and a large and varied selection of unusual gifts.

Next door is Meander Boutique: Who cater for the ladies, with an excellent range of clothes, along with footwear, knitwear, jewellery and other accessories.

Then Spencer-Coleman SCFA: A shop that sells mainly contemporary paintings, also a range of glassware.

At the end is, Gerard's Unisex Hair Studio and Beauty parlour: They specialise in designer cutting, facials, pedicure/manicure, waxing, massaging, tanning and much more.

On the right hand side, there is the managerial side with the executive offices, two boardrooms. Secretarial services, photocopying and computer access. The first floor has a sixty seater conference room with full projection and audio visual facilities. A foyer area, with toilets and a small bar. The centre is also used by, local organisations and clubs.

The George is now into it's second Millennium and continues to play a very active role.
Still serving superb food and a personal service rarely found these days, making the hotel, a memorable place to stay.
The Business complex, with all its resources available for the businessmen, local clubs and associations is very much in demand.

I am confident that the George of Stamford will continue with its service par excellence, for aeons.

Taking advantage of the late summer to enjoy lunch in the courtyard.

You will find a convival and relaxed atmosphere taking lunch in the Garden Restaurant.

The colour and calmness of the Monastery garden.